MANDALA ADULT COLORING BOOK

Stress-Relieving Designs: Mandalas, Flowers, Butterflies, Doodle Patterns, Floral Patterns, Decorative Designs, Coloring for Adults

By

Amber Emerson

©2018

Copyright notice

Stress-Relieving Designs: Mandalas, Flowers, Butterflies, Doodle

Patterns, Floral Patterns, Decorative Designs, Coloring for Adults

Use this book as a tool to rediscover your inner child and find peace in our turbulent world of strife and chaos

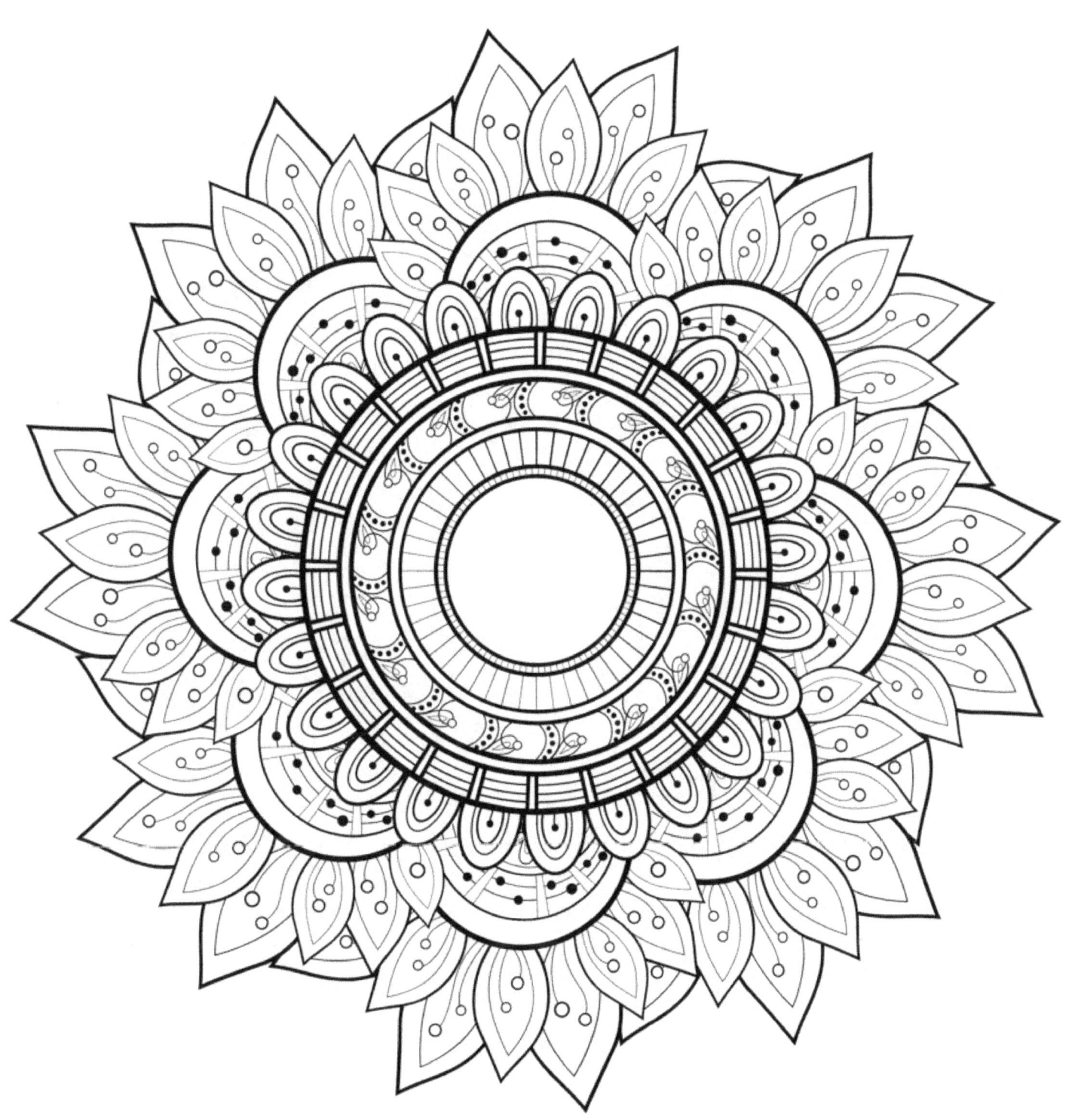

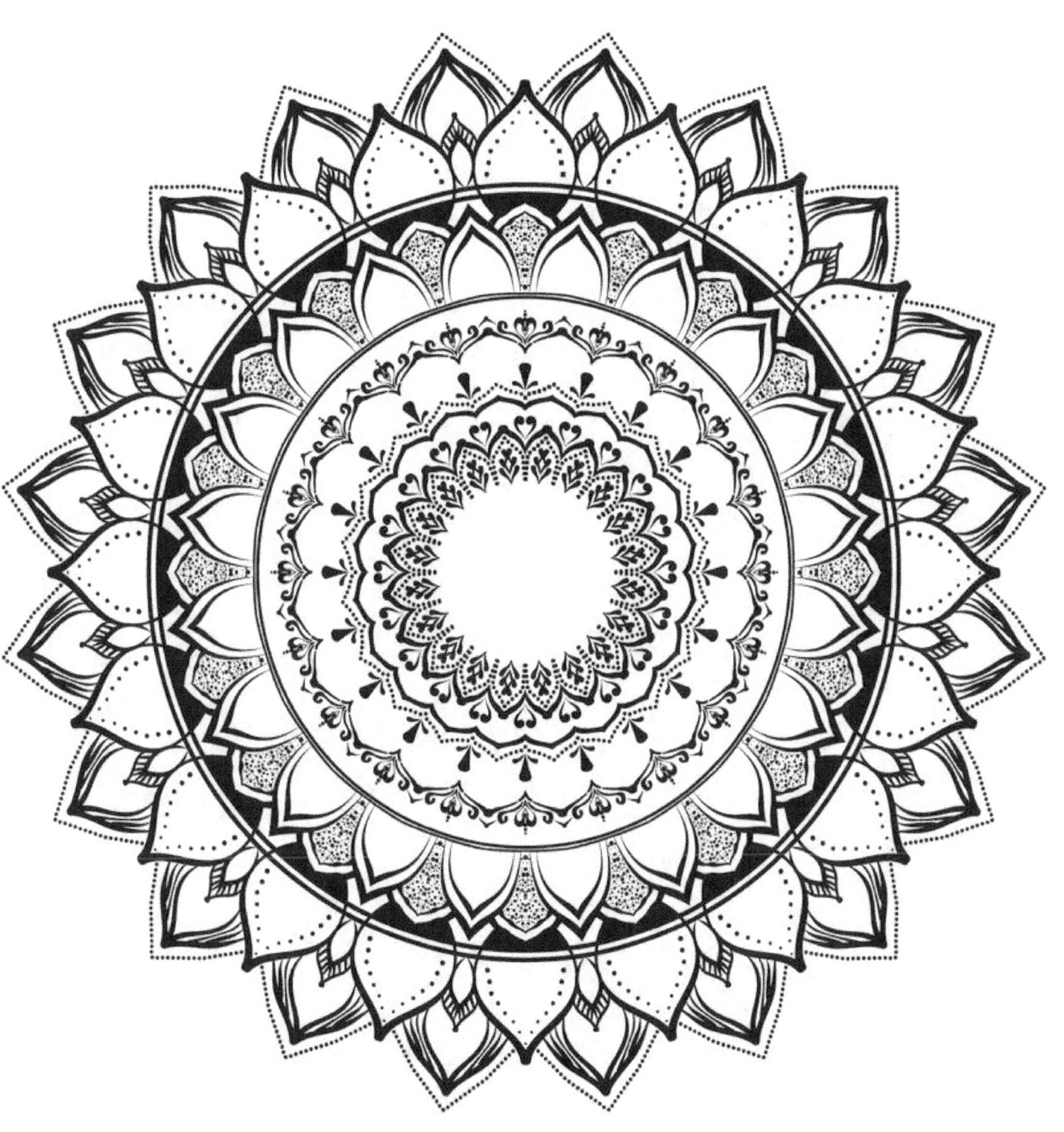

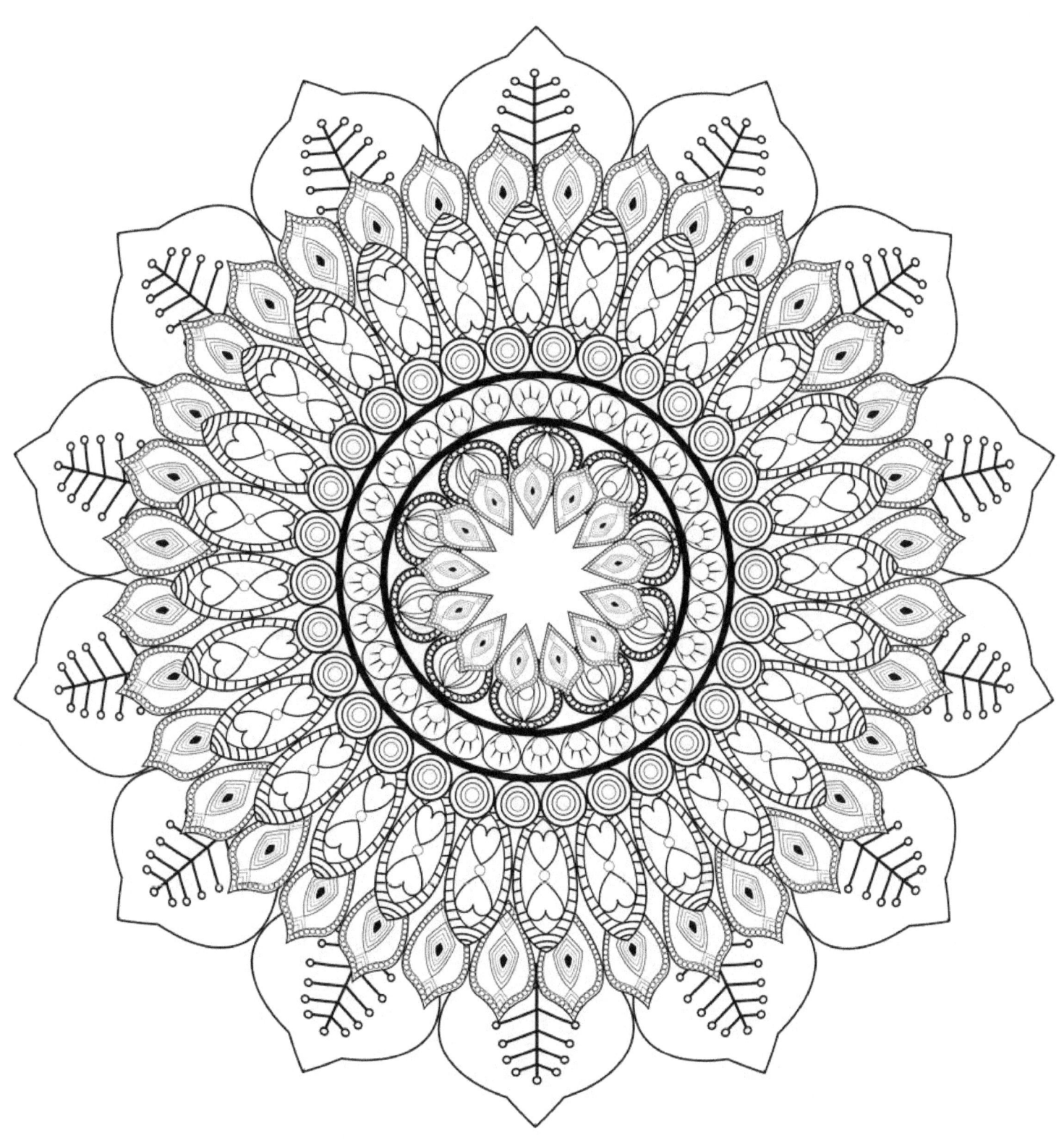

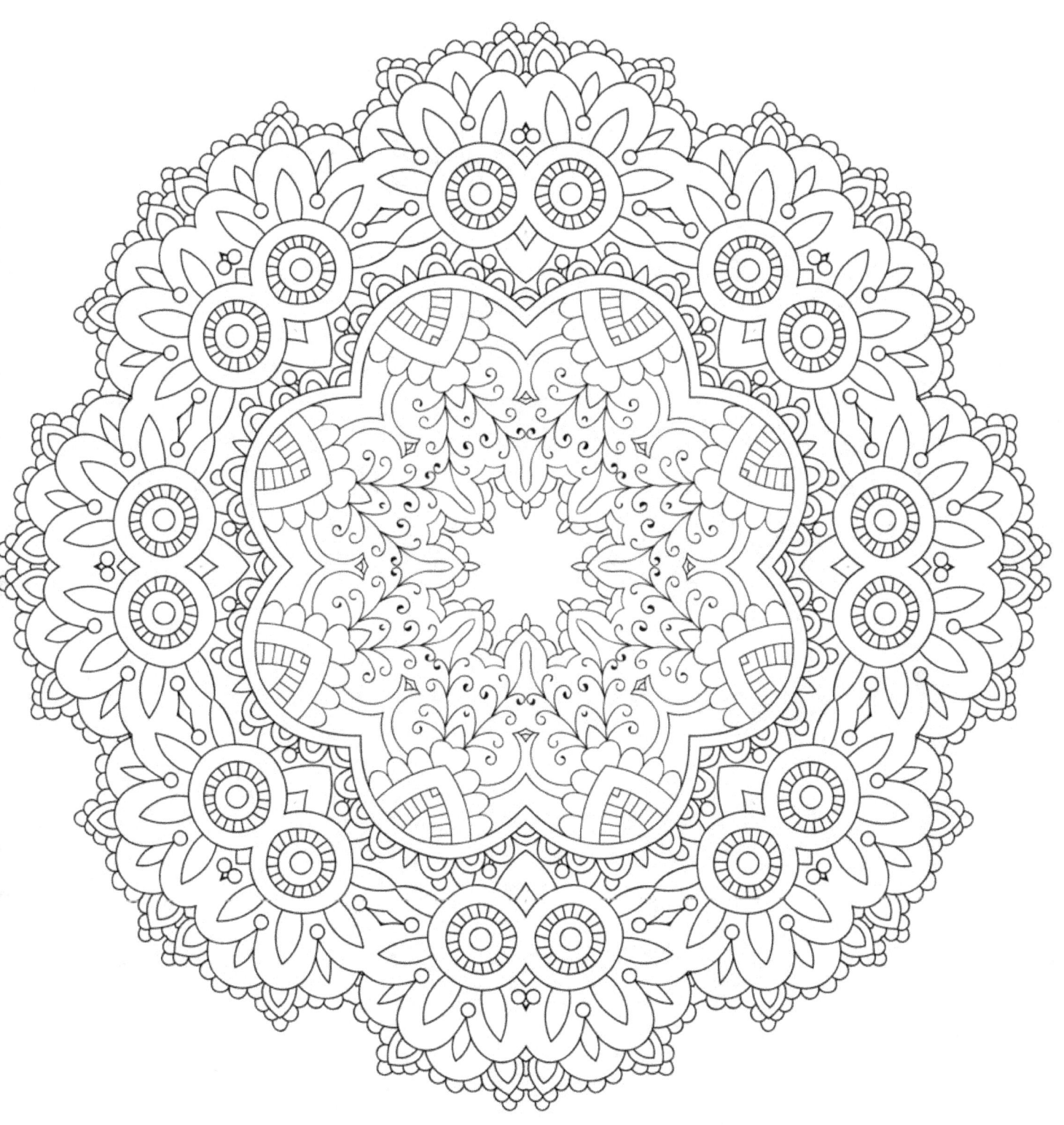

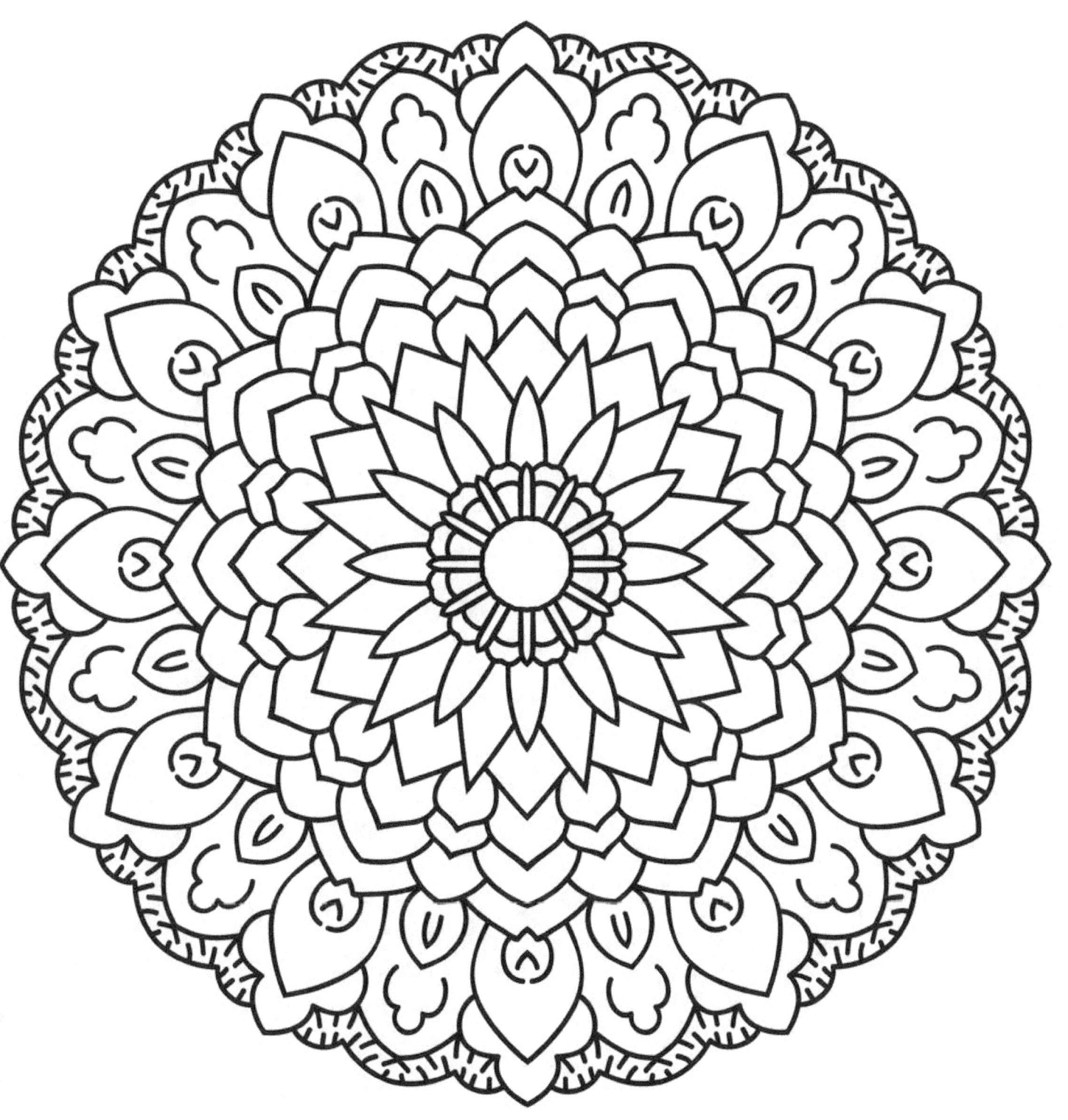

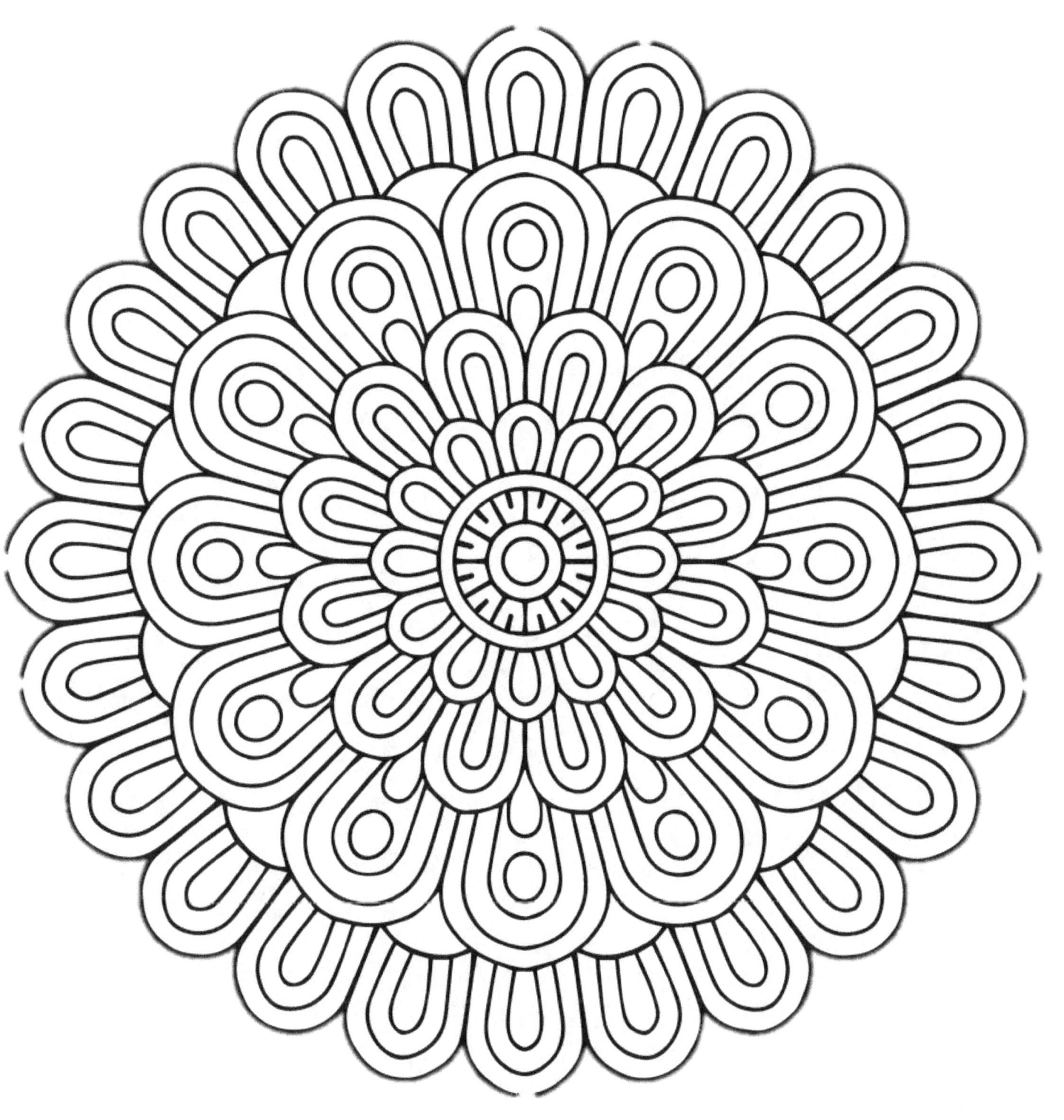

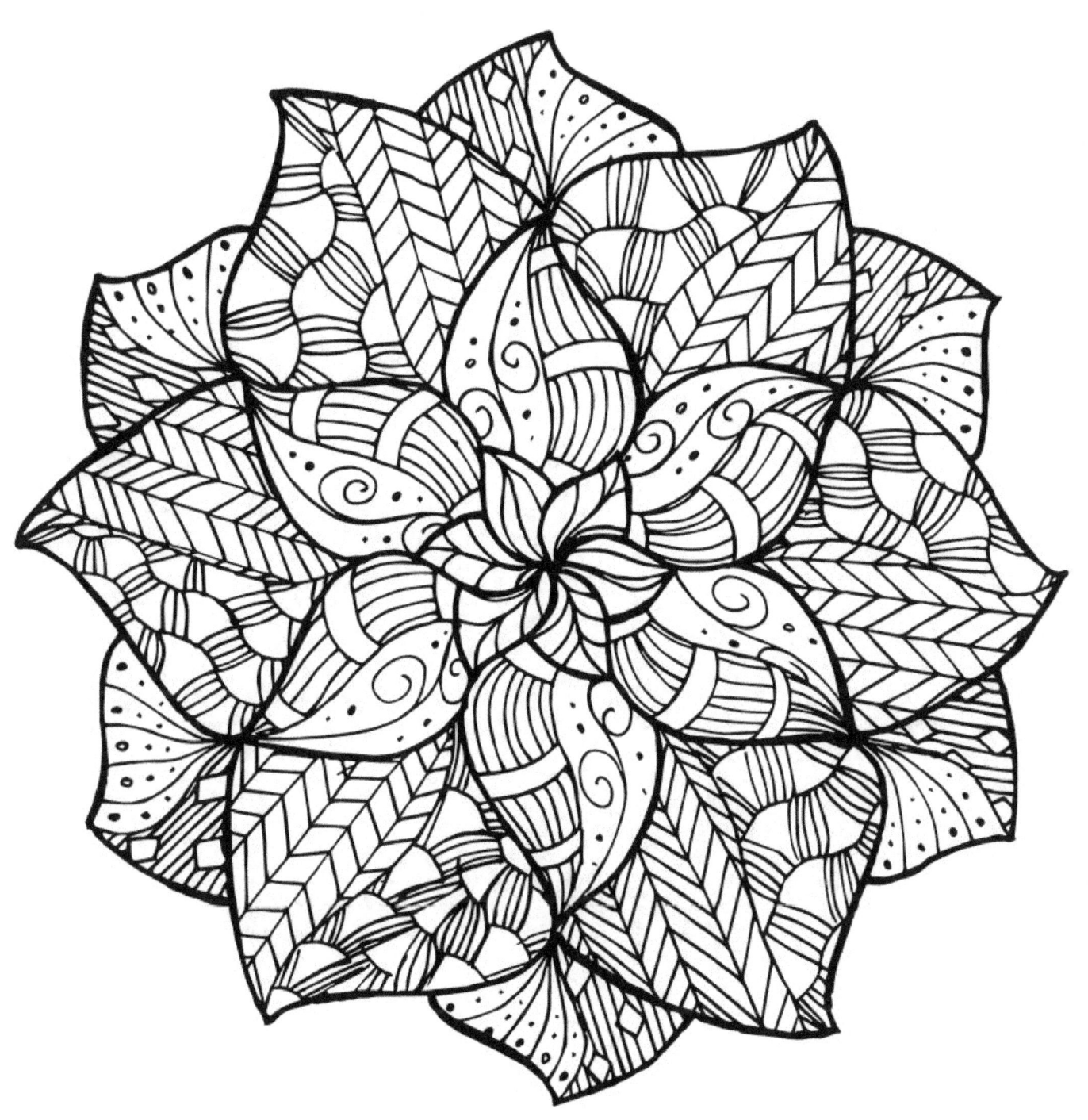

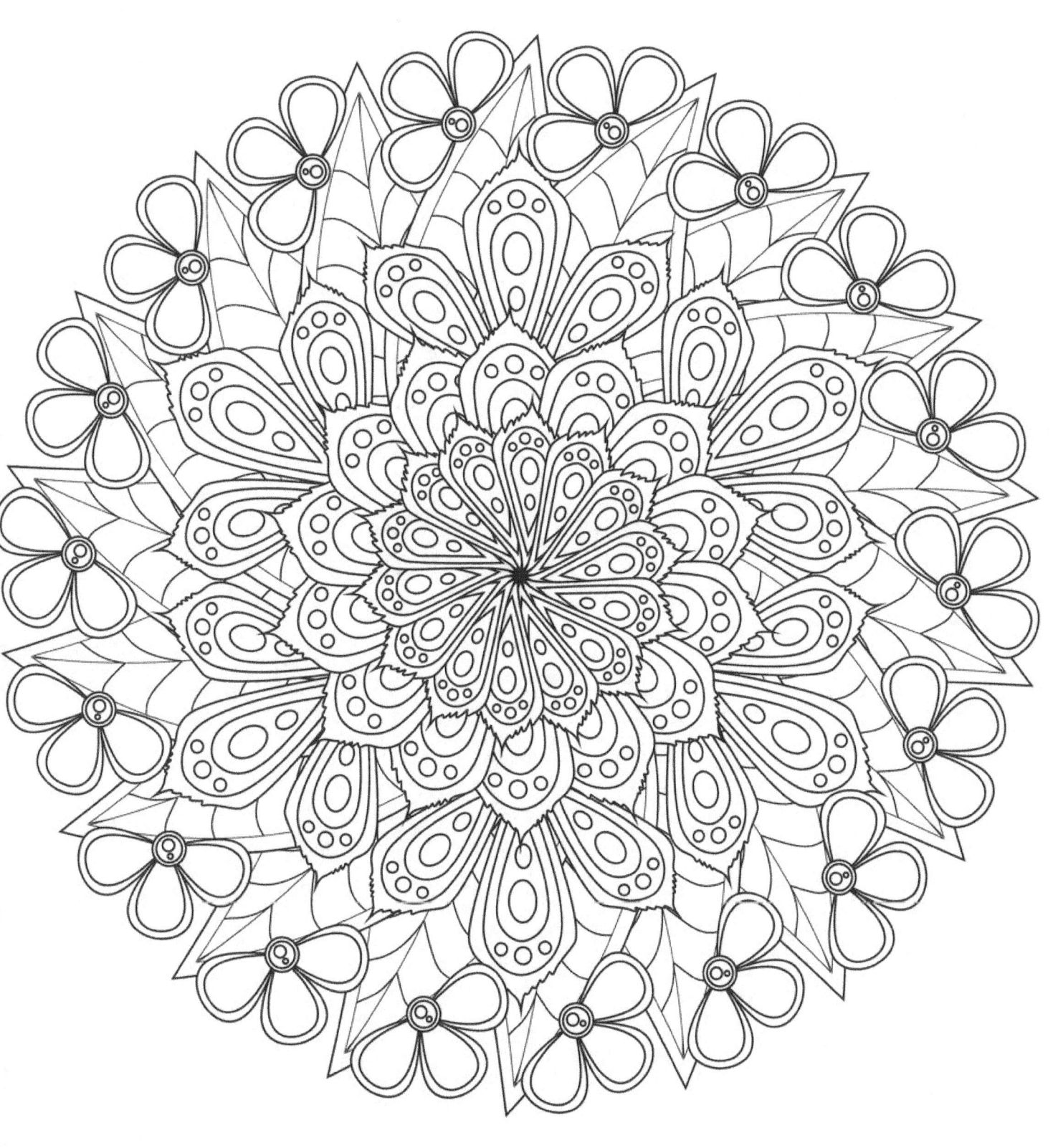

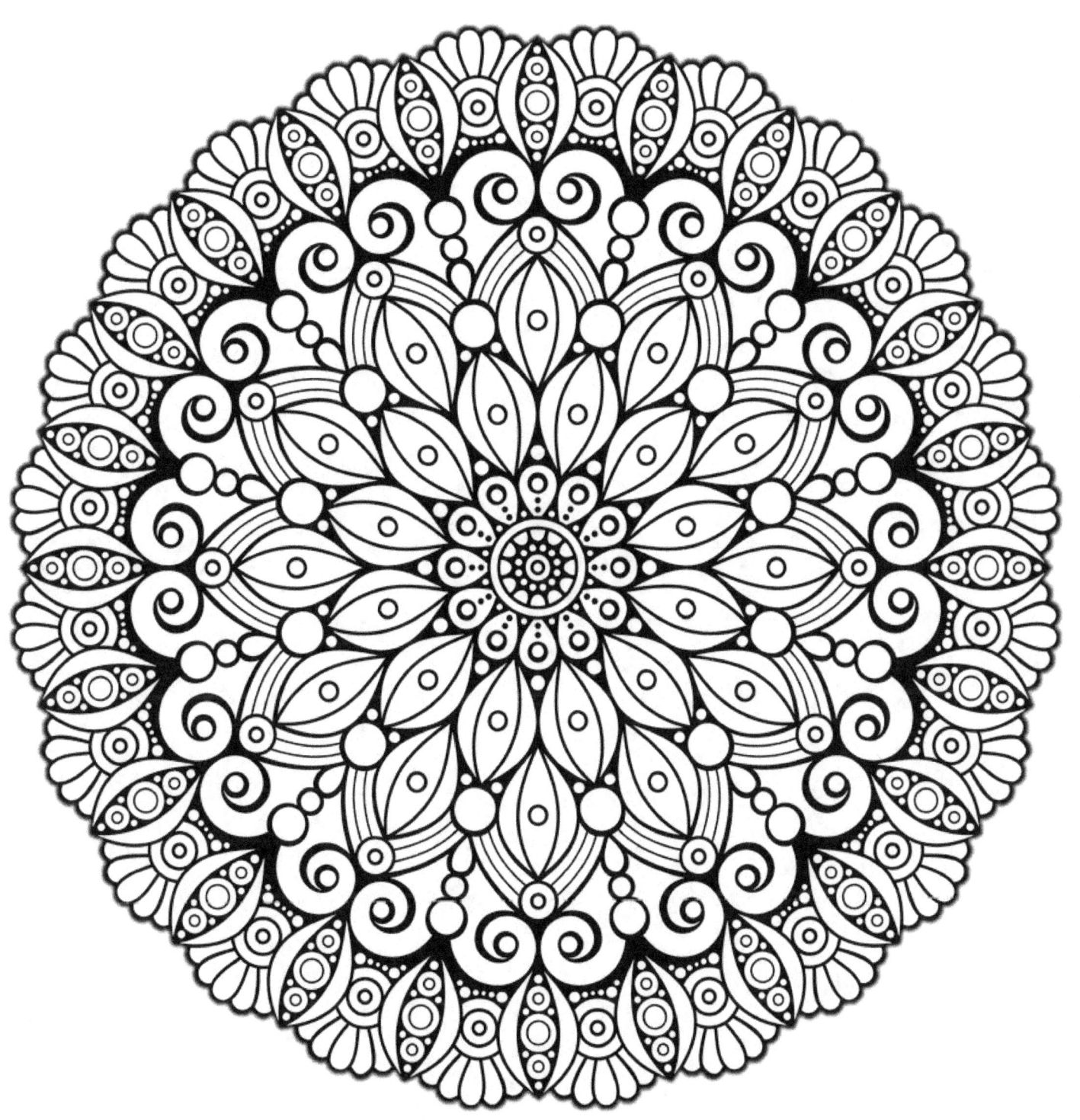

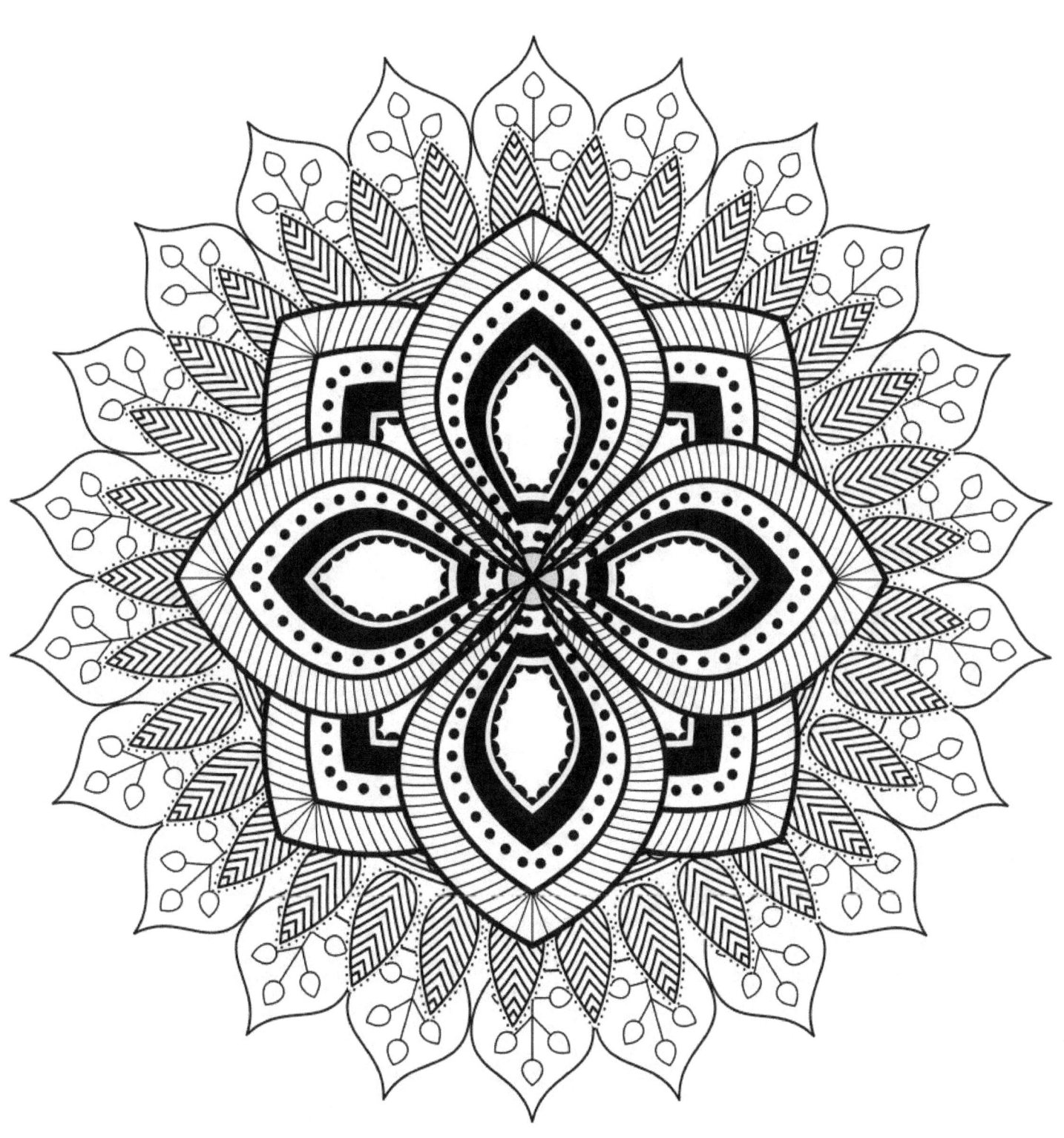

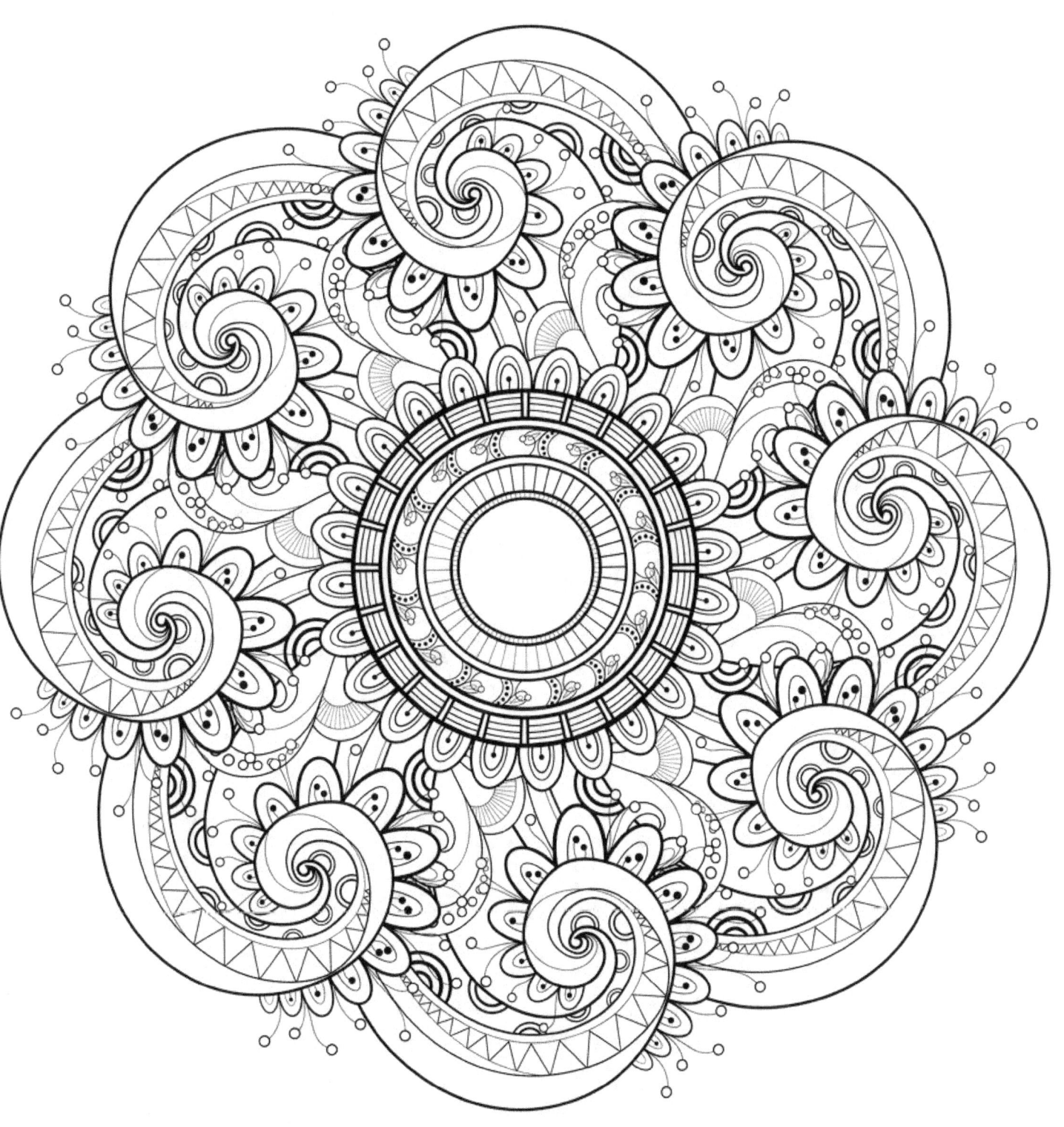

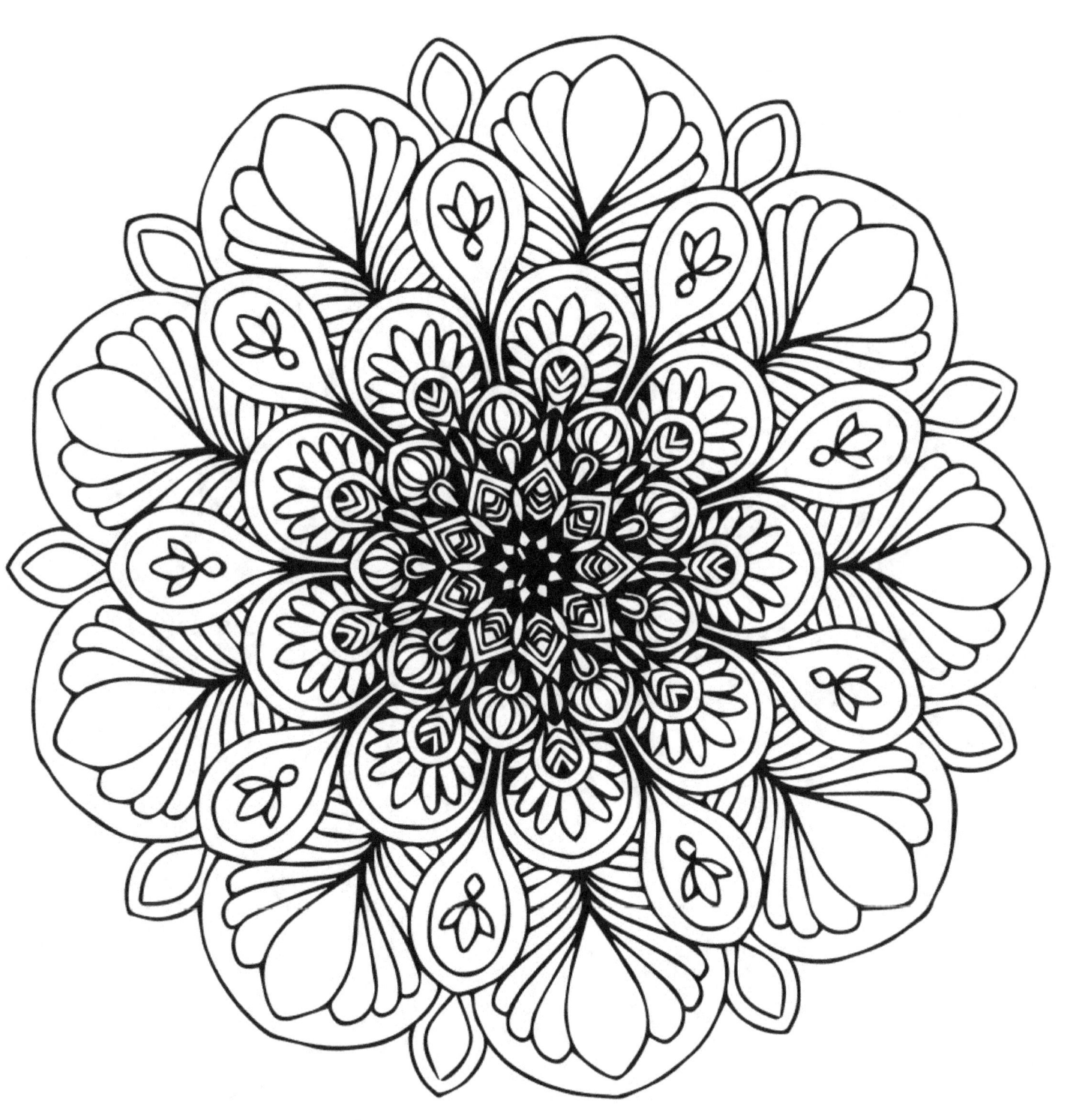

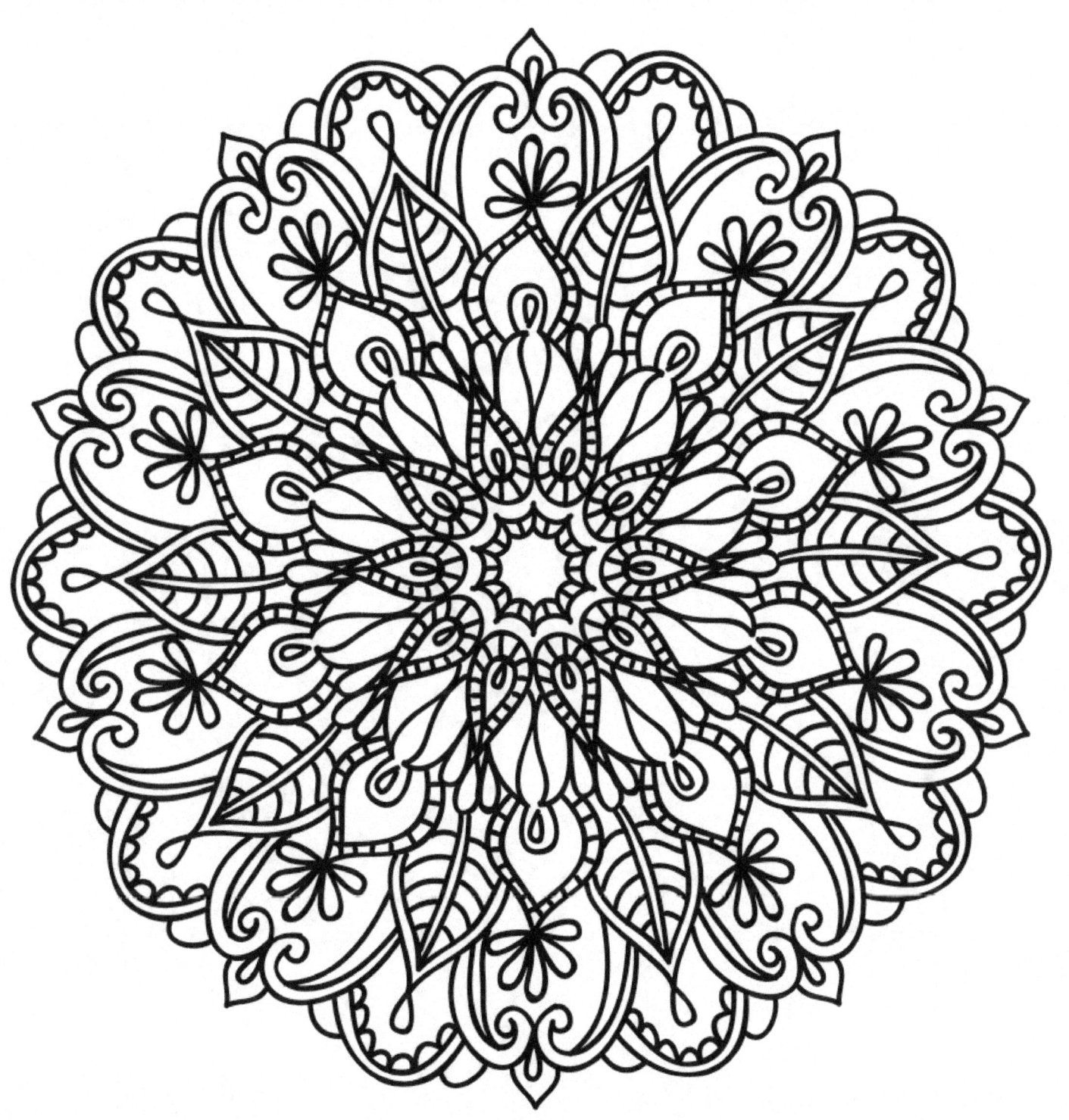

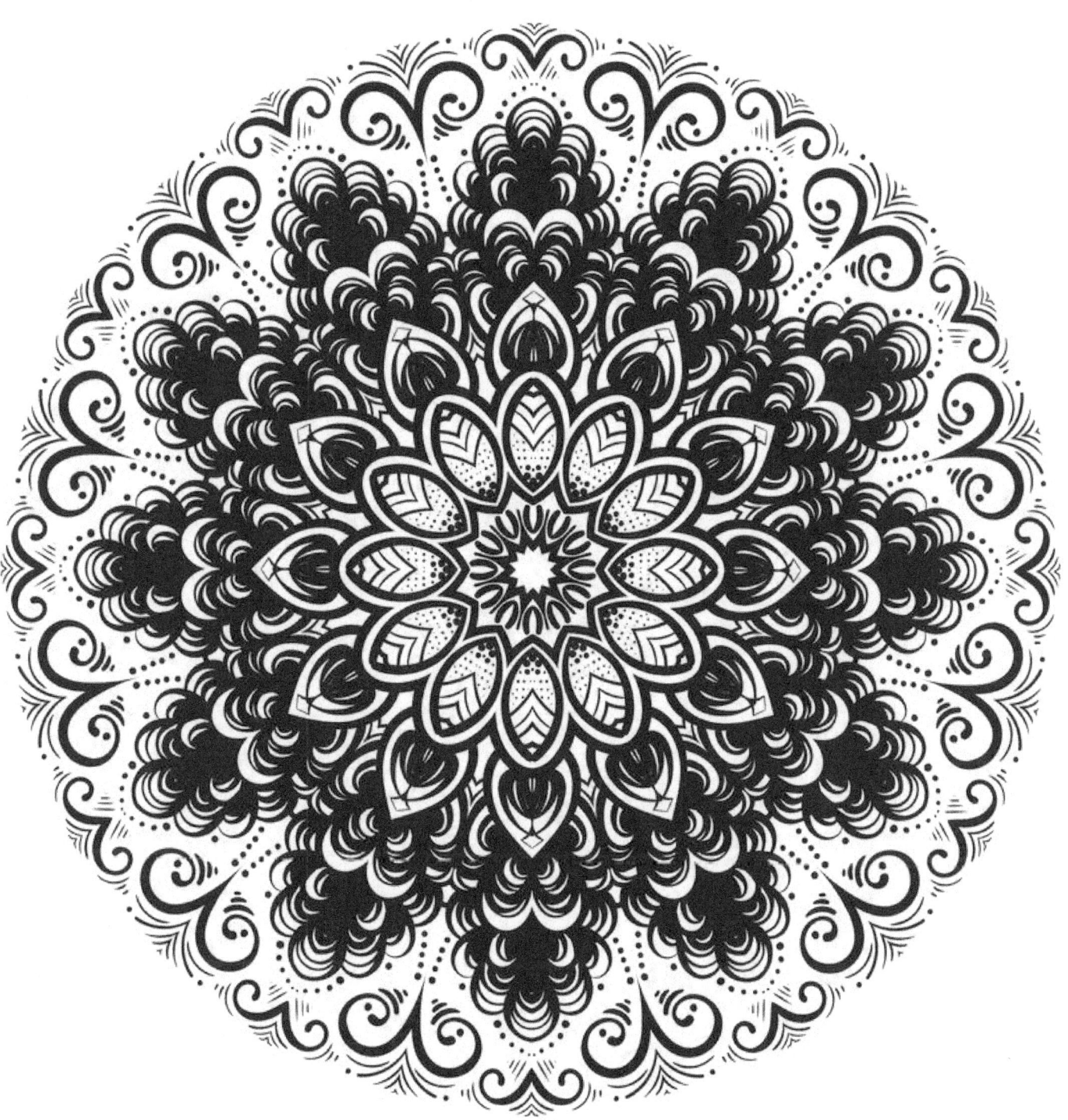

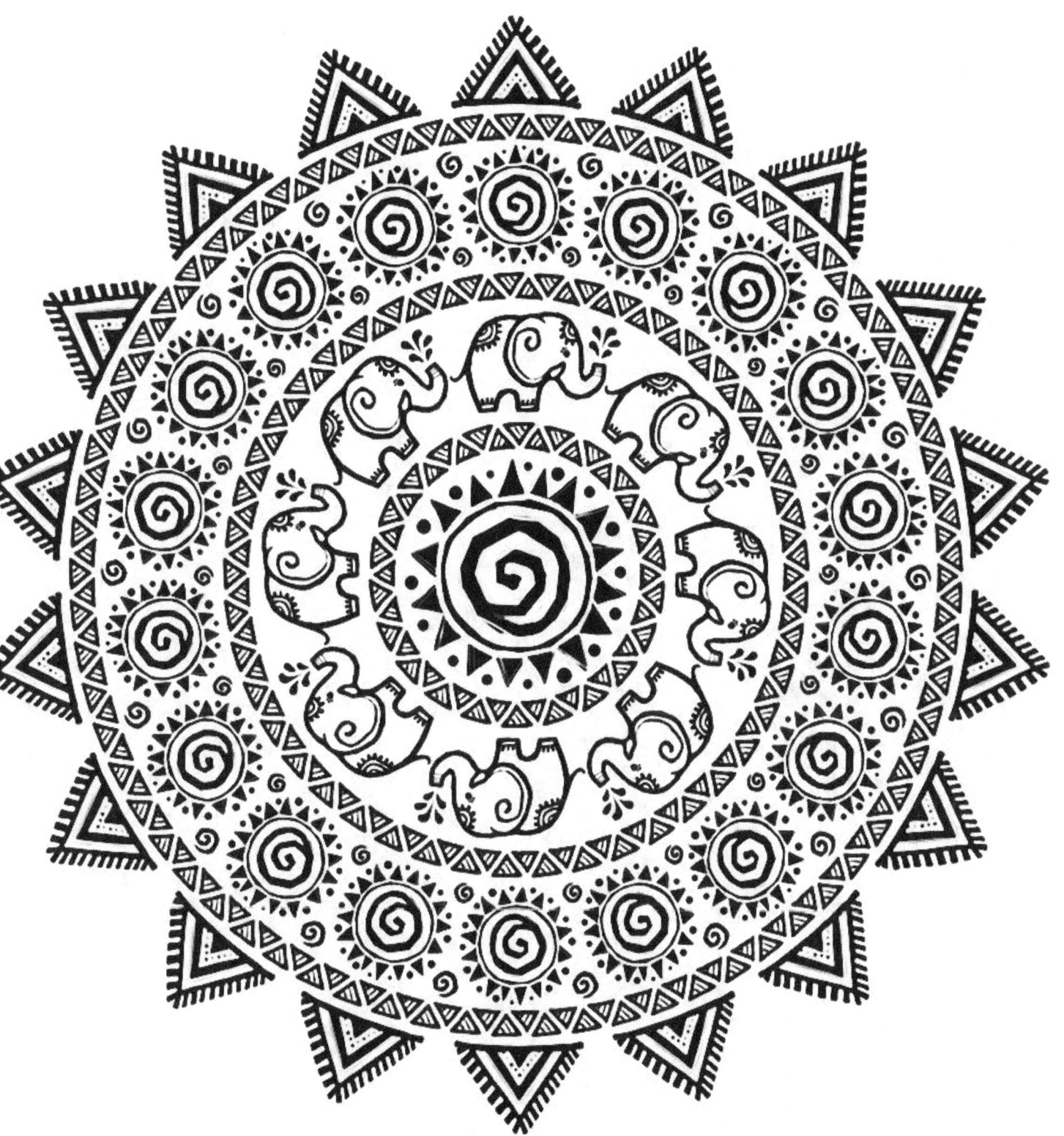

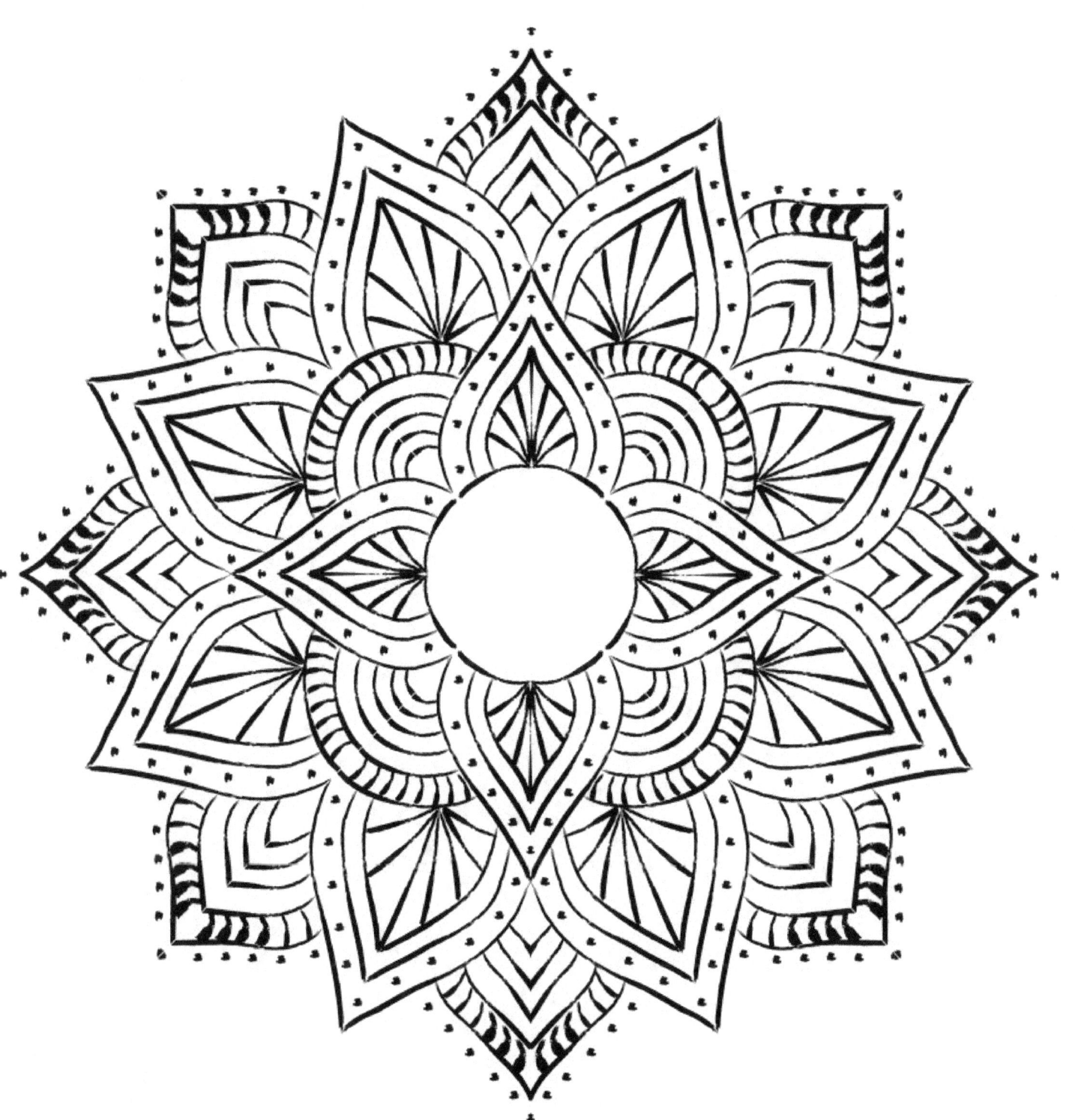

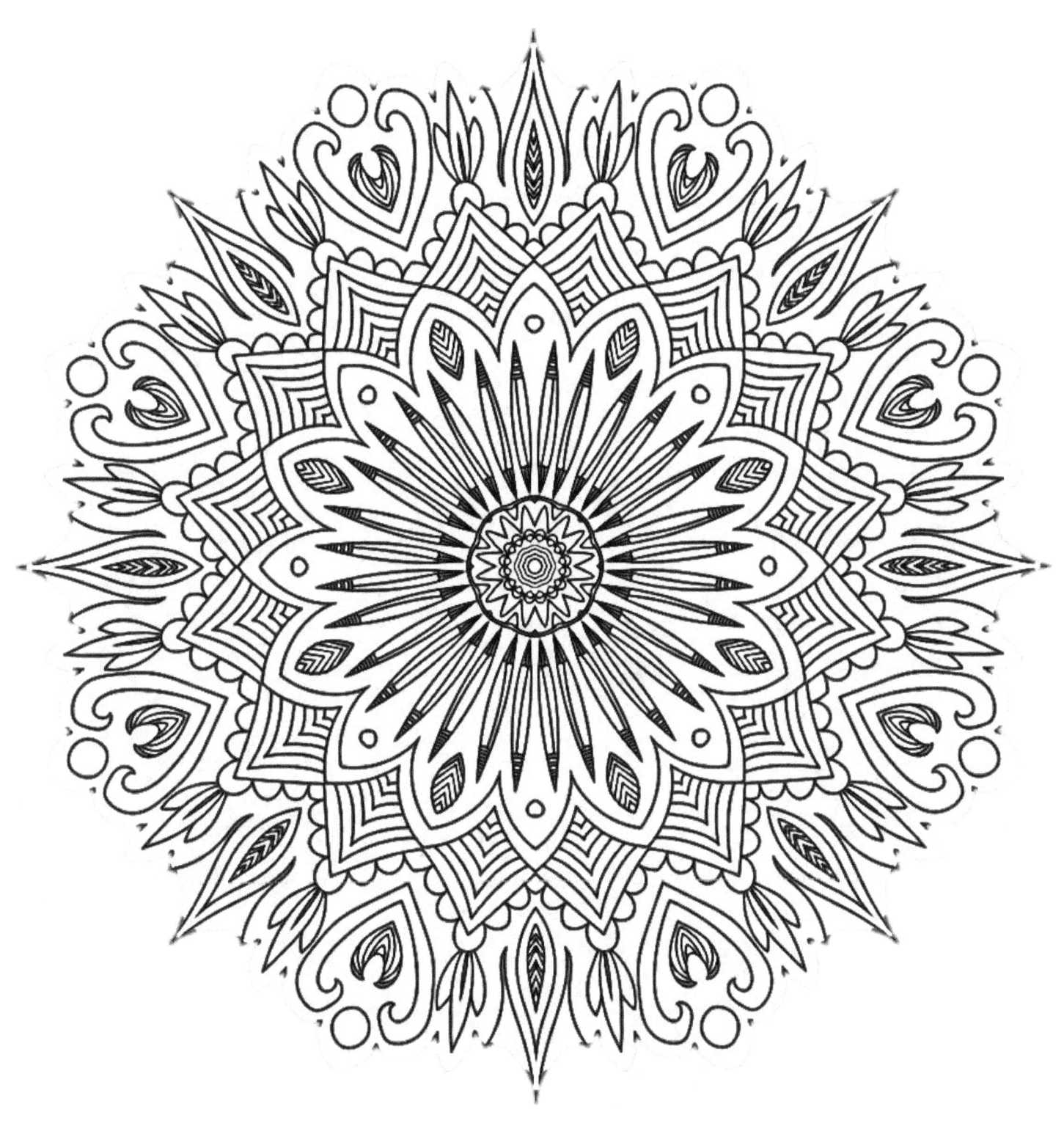

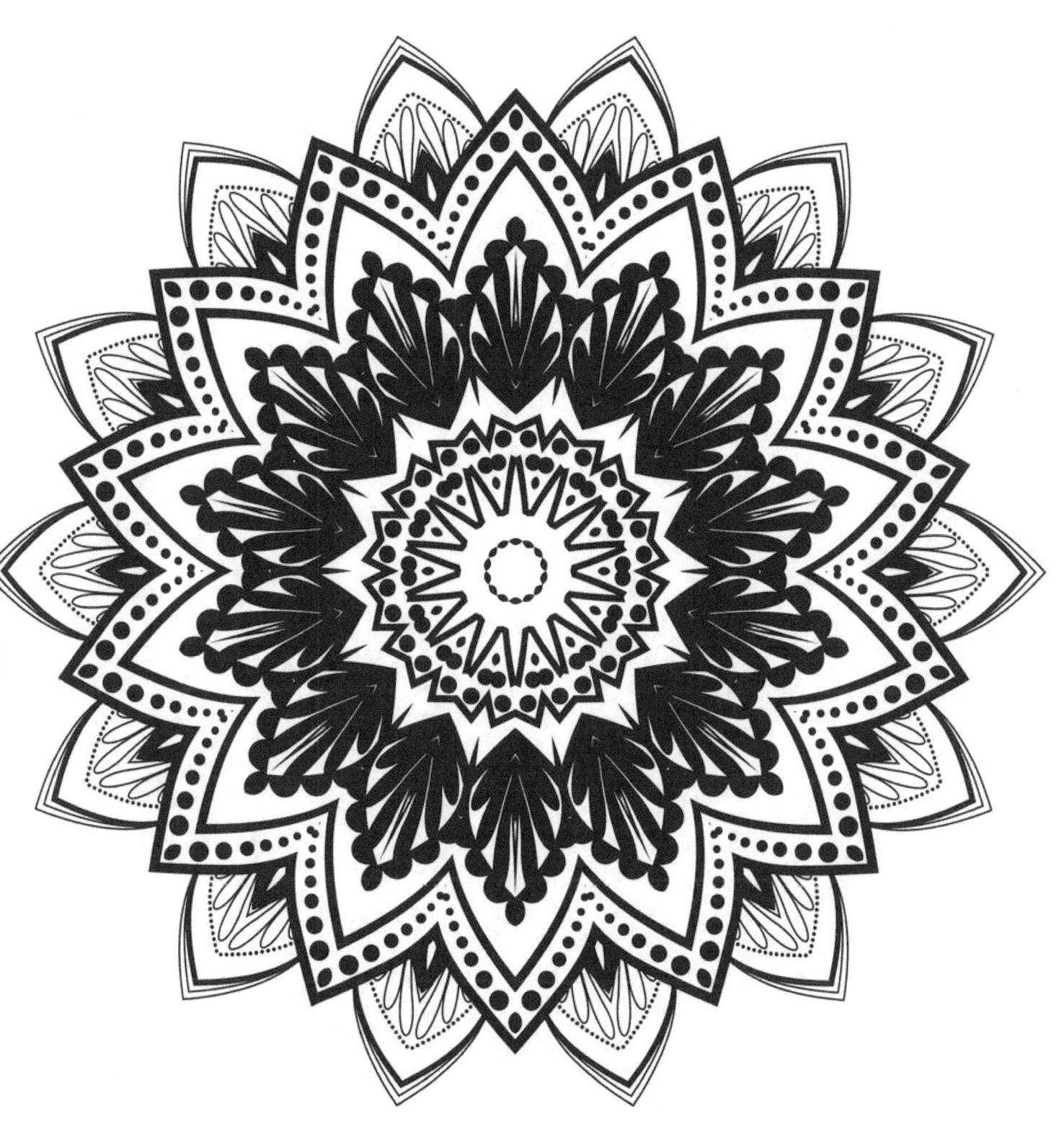

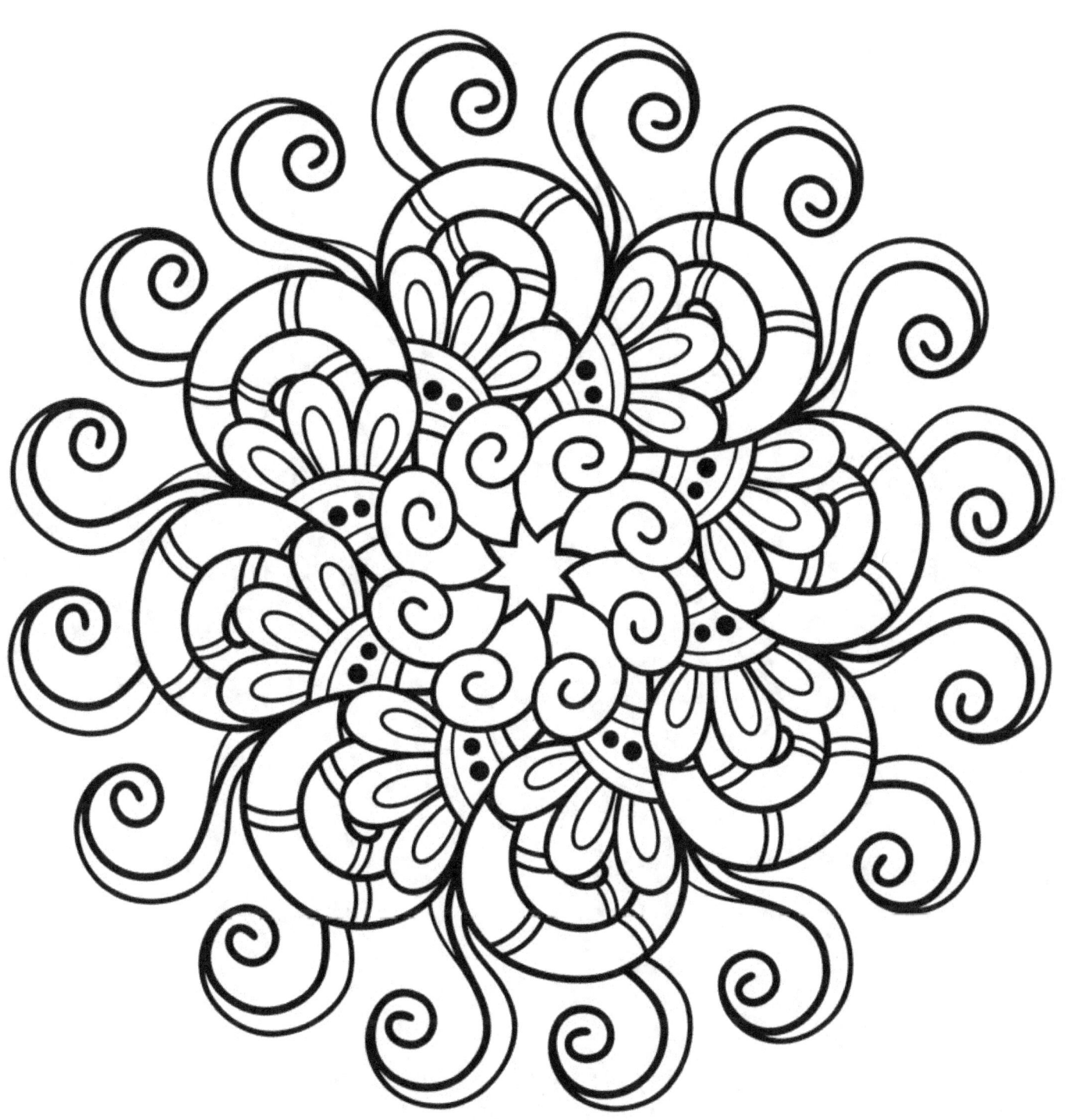

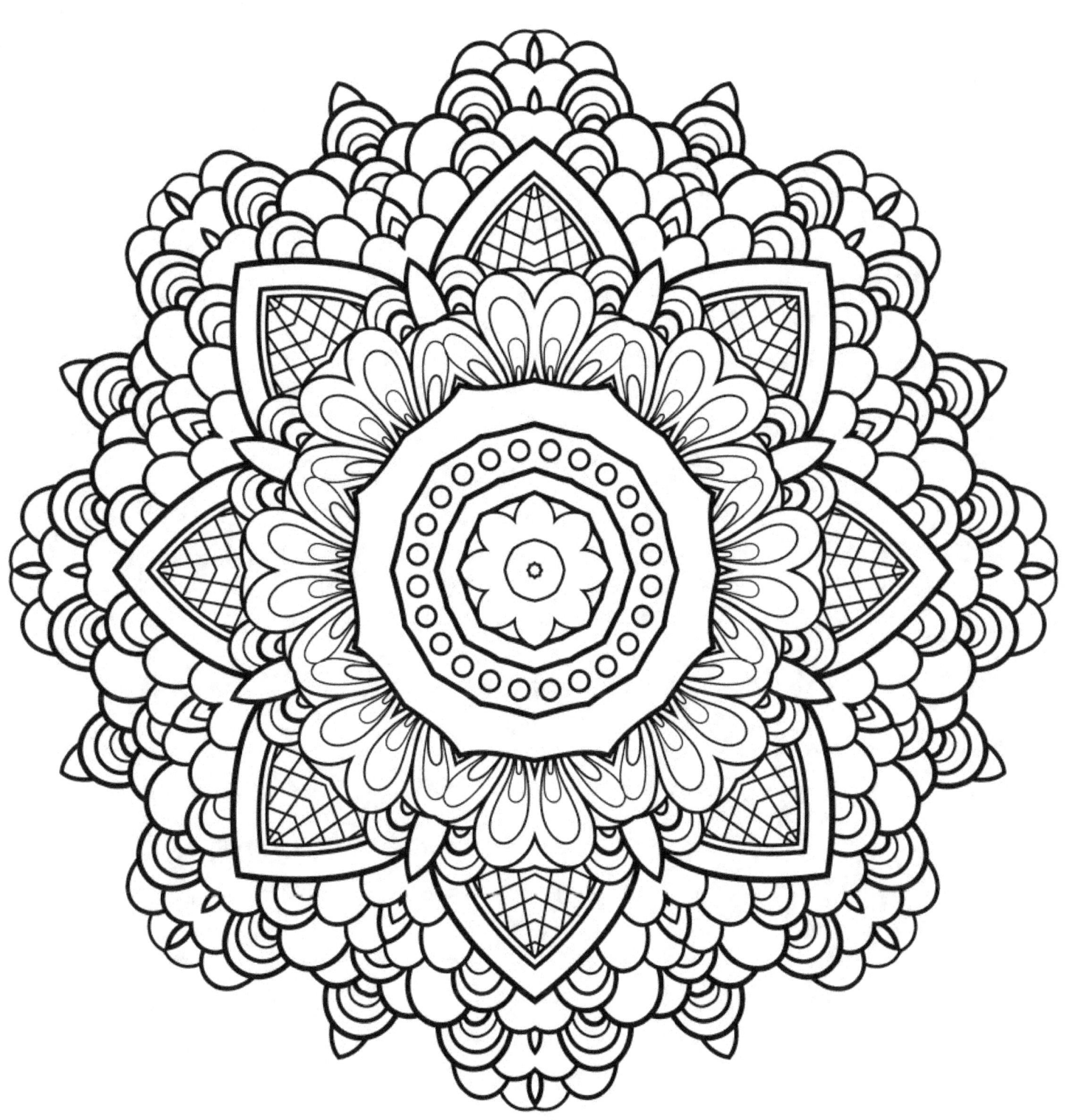

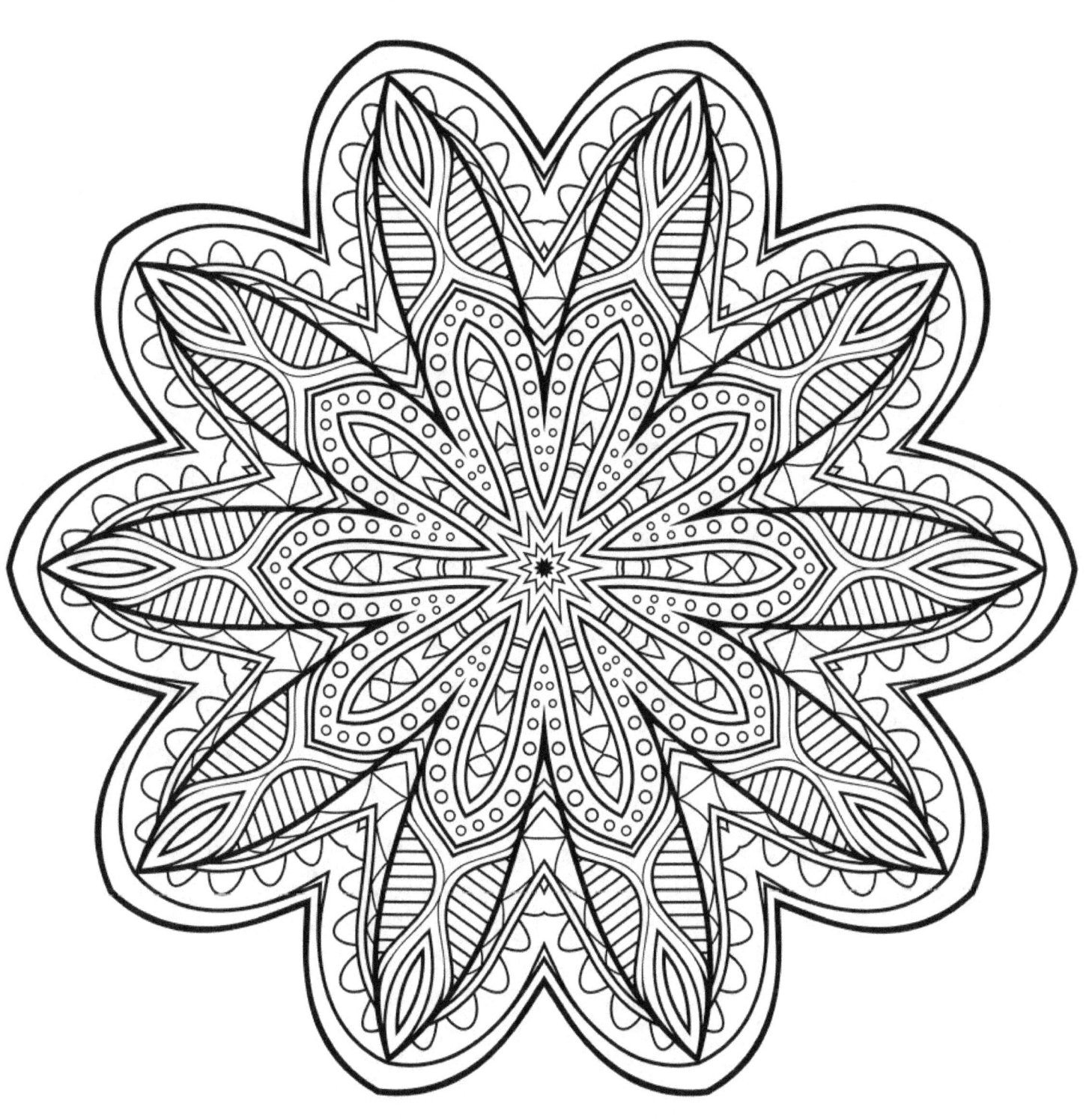

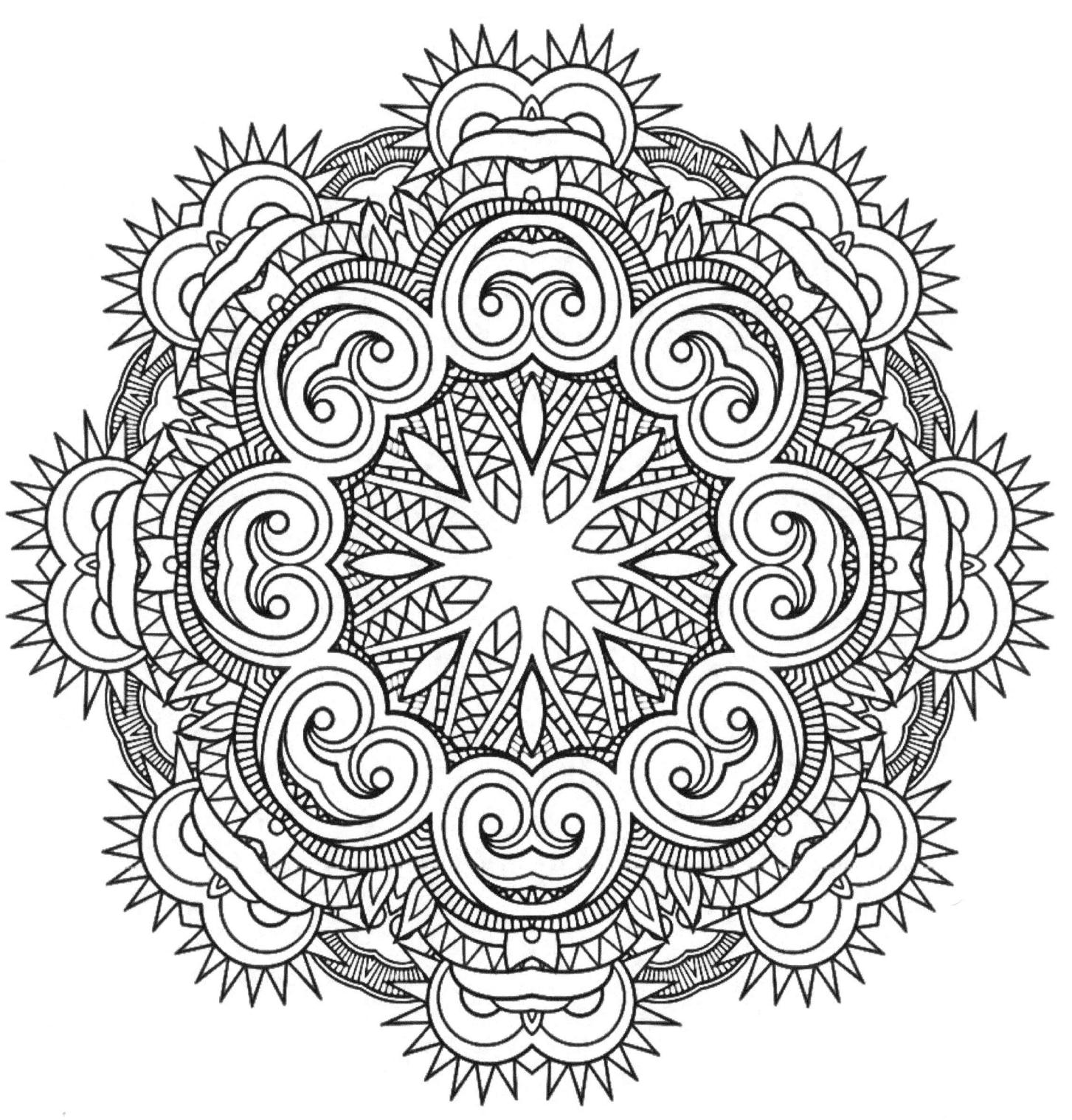

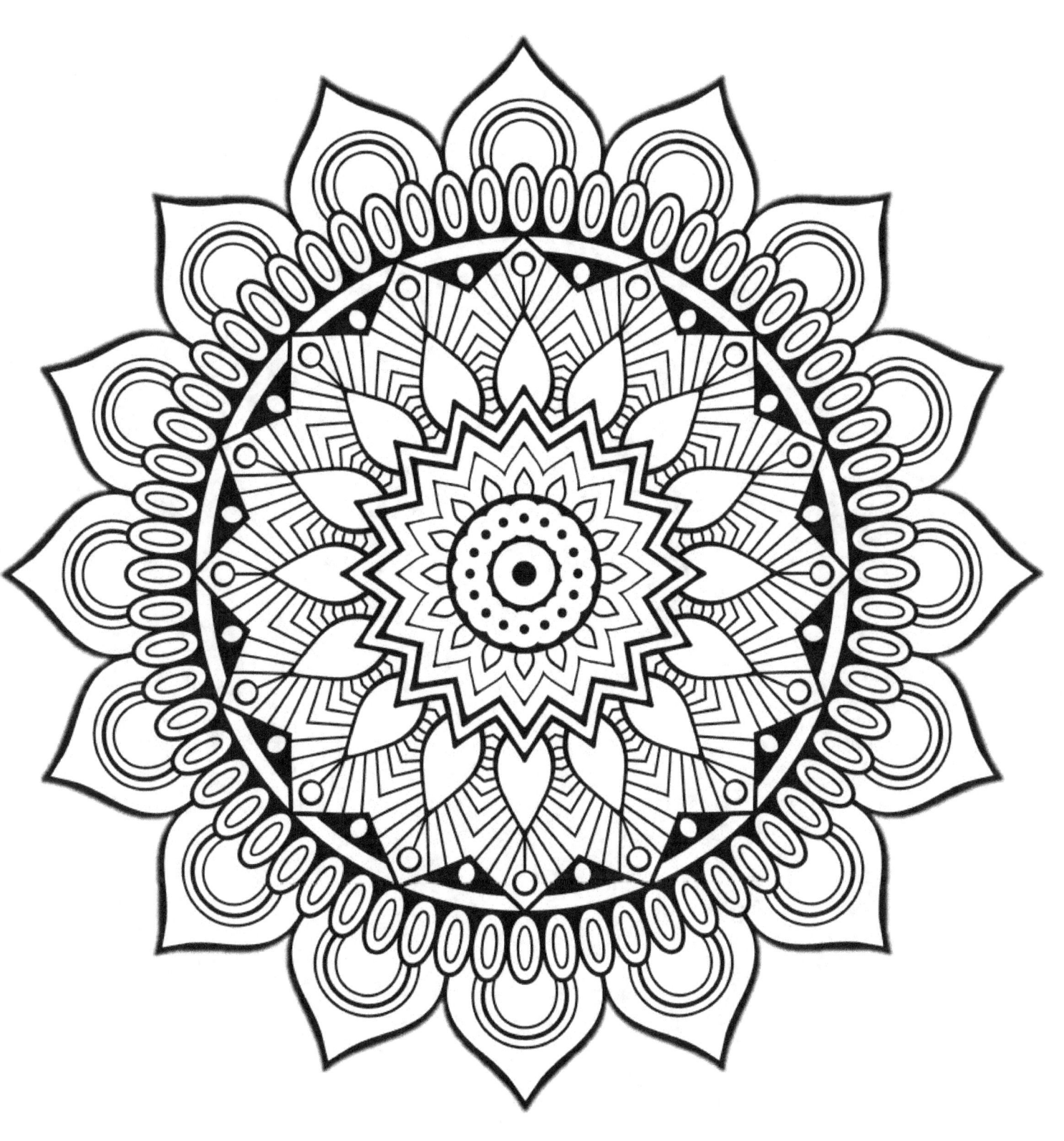

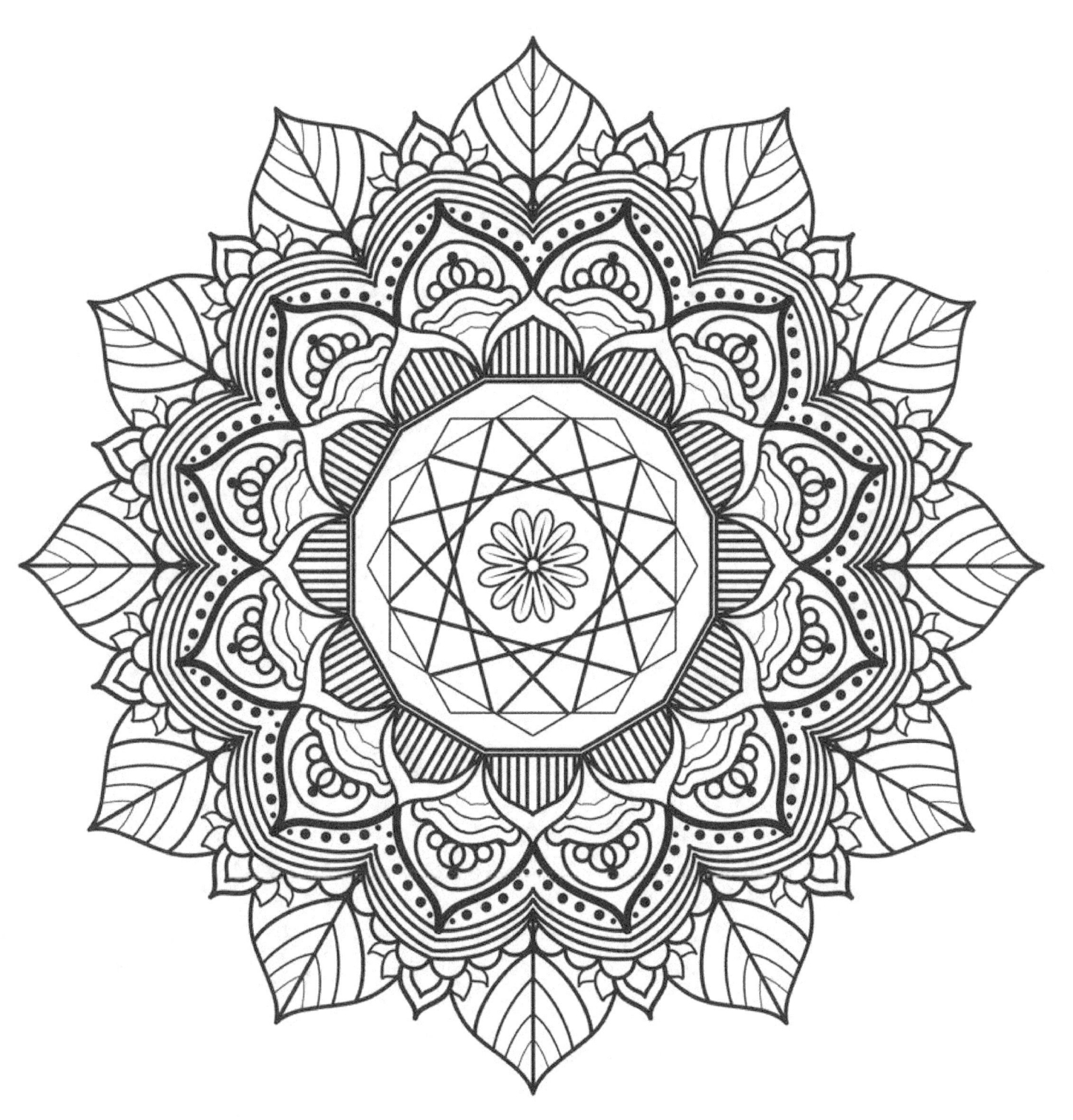

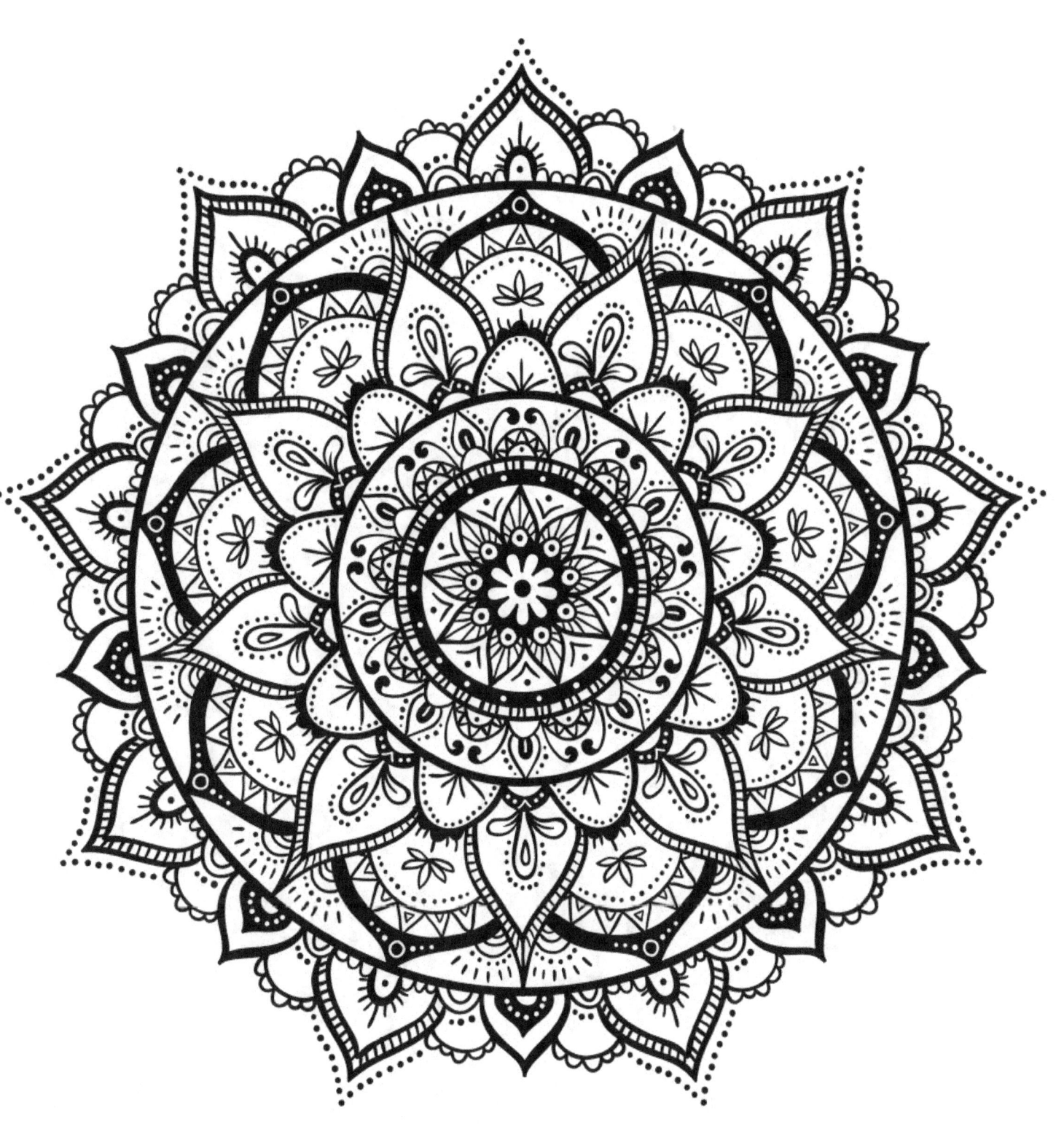

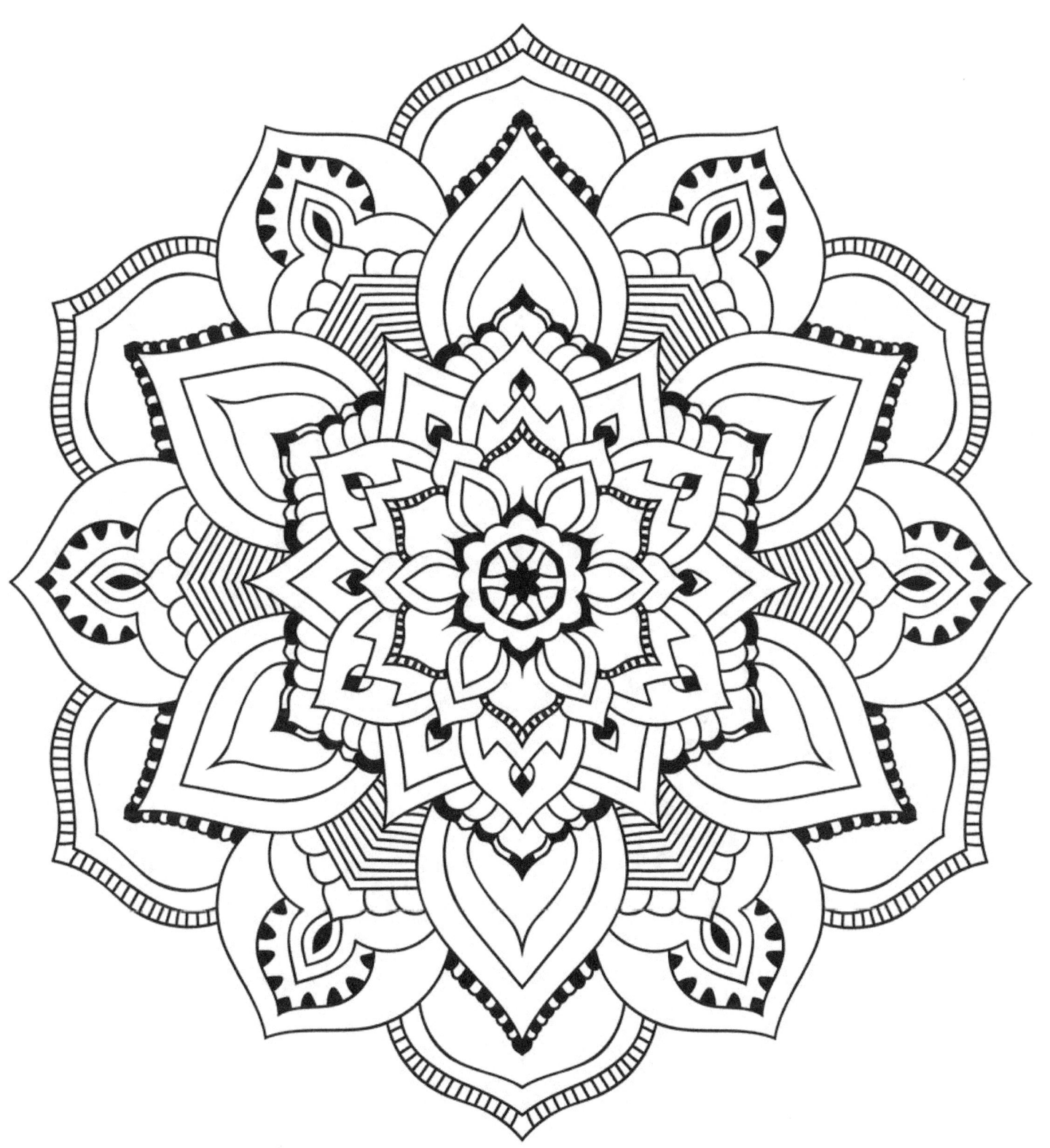

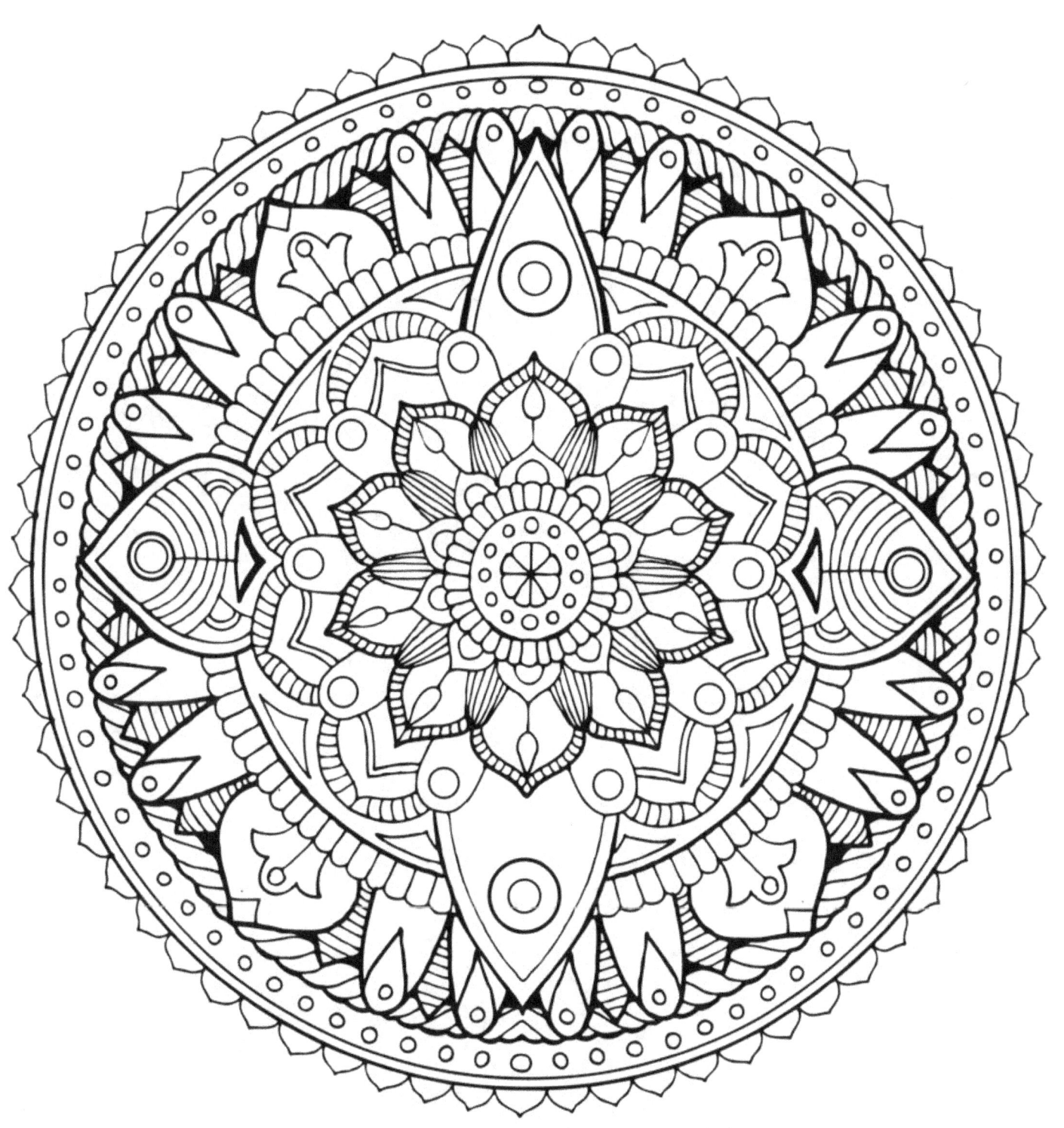

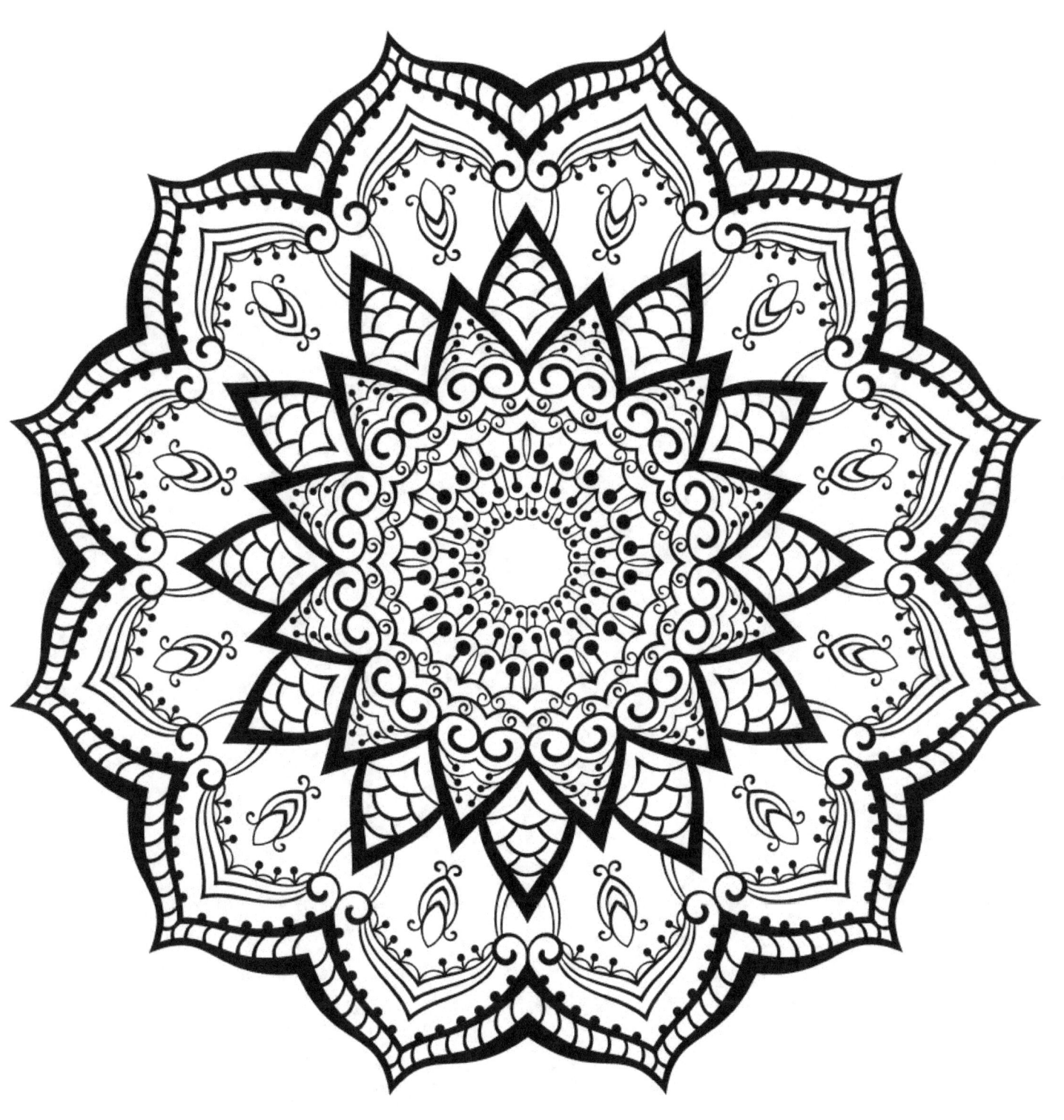

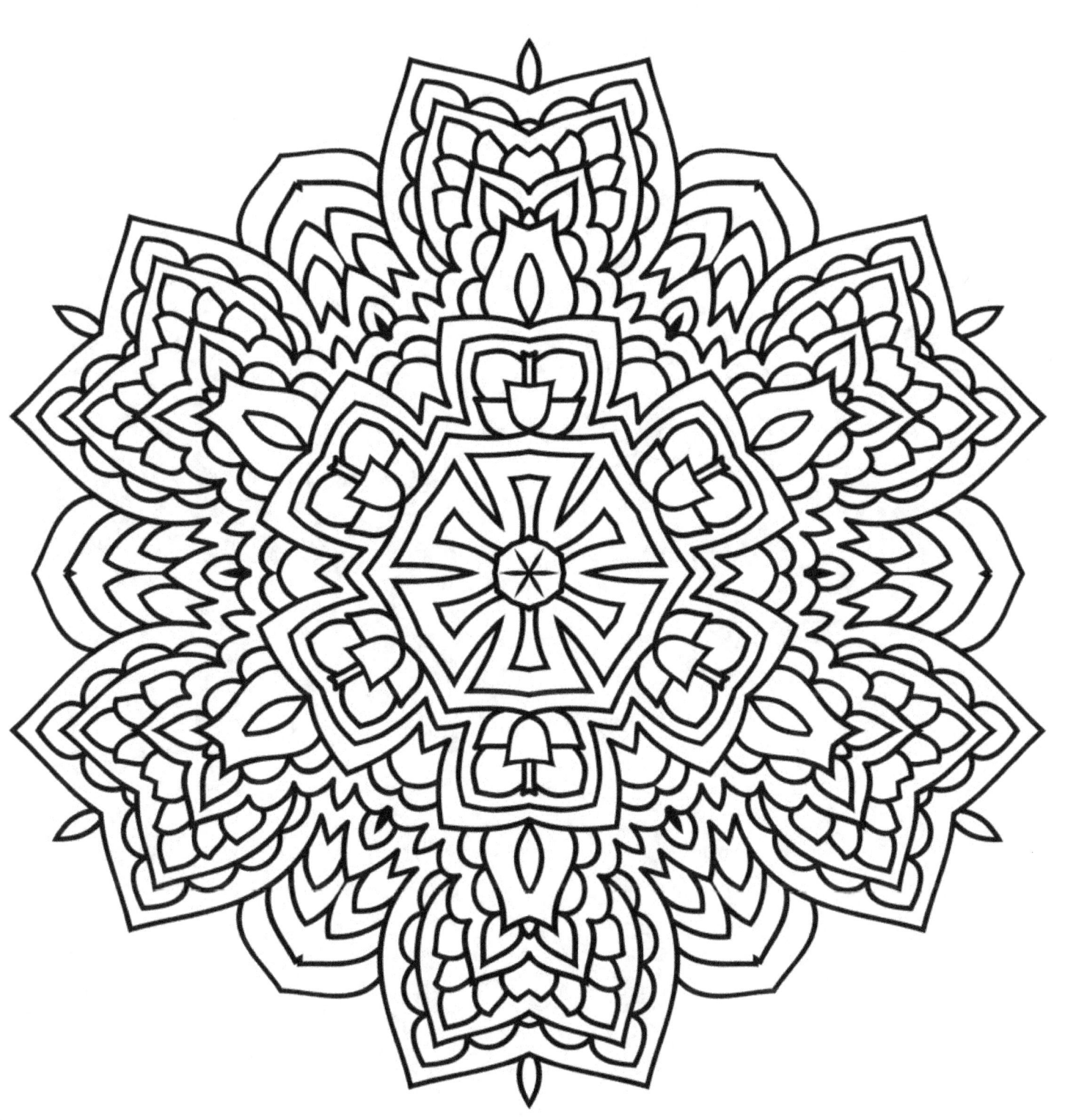

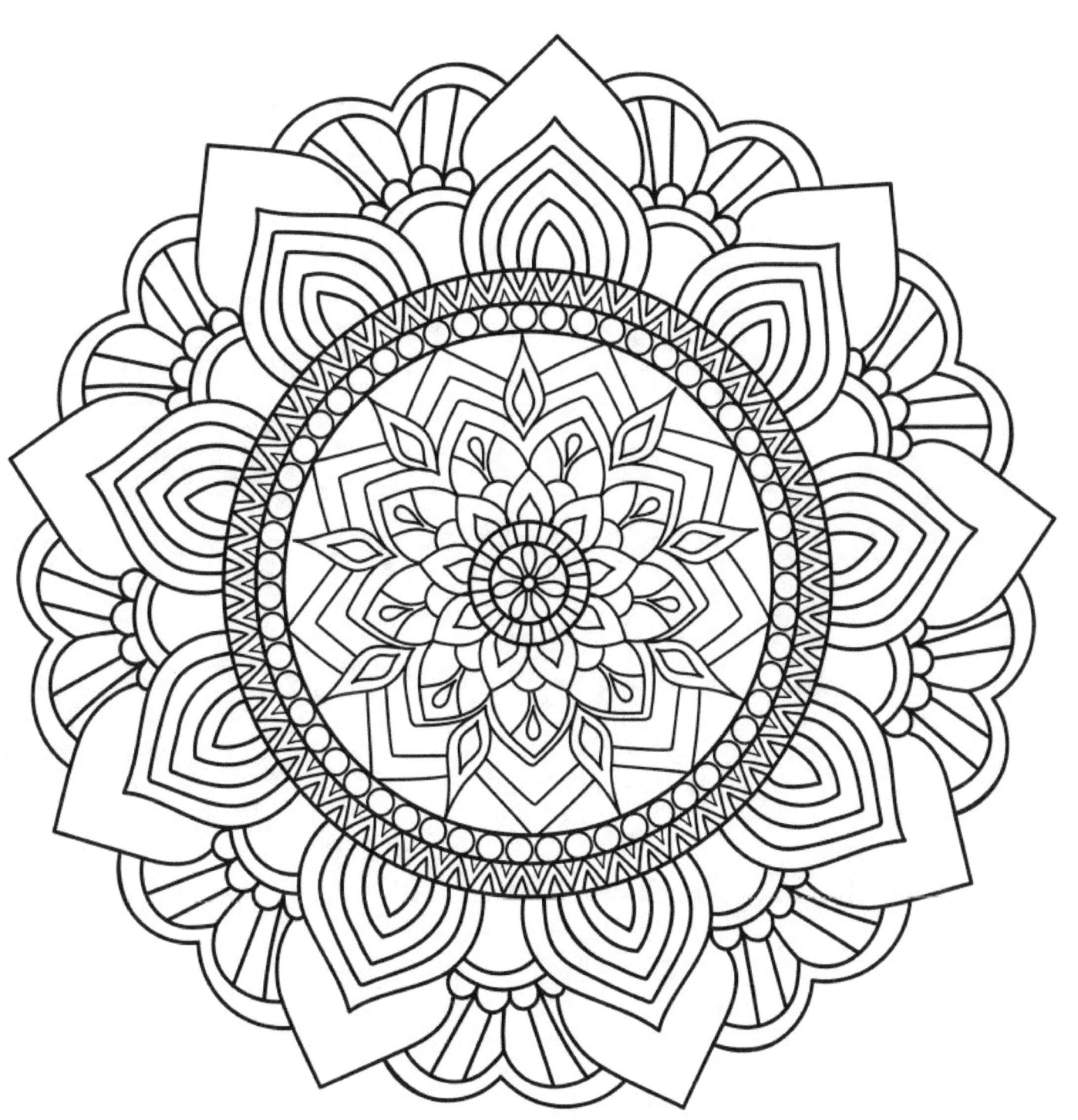

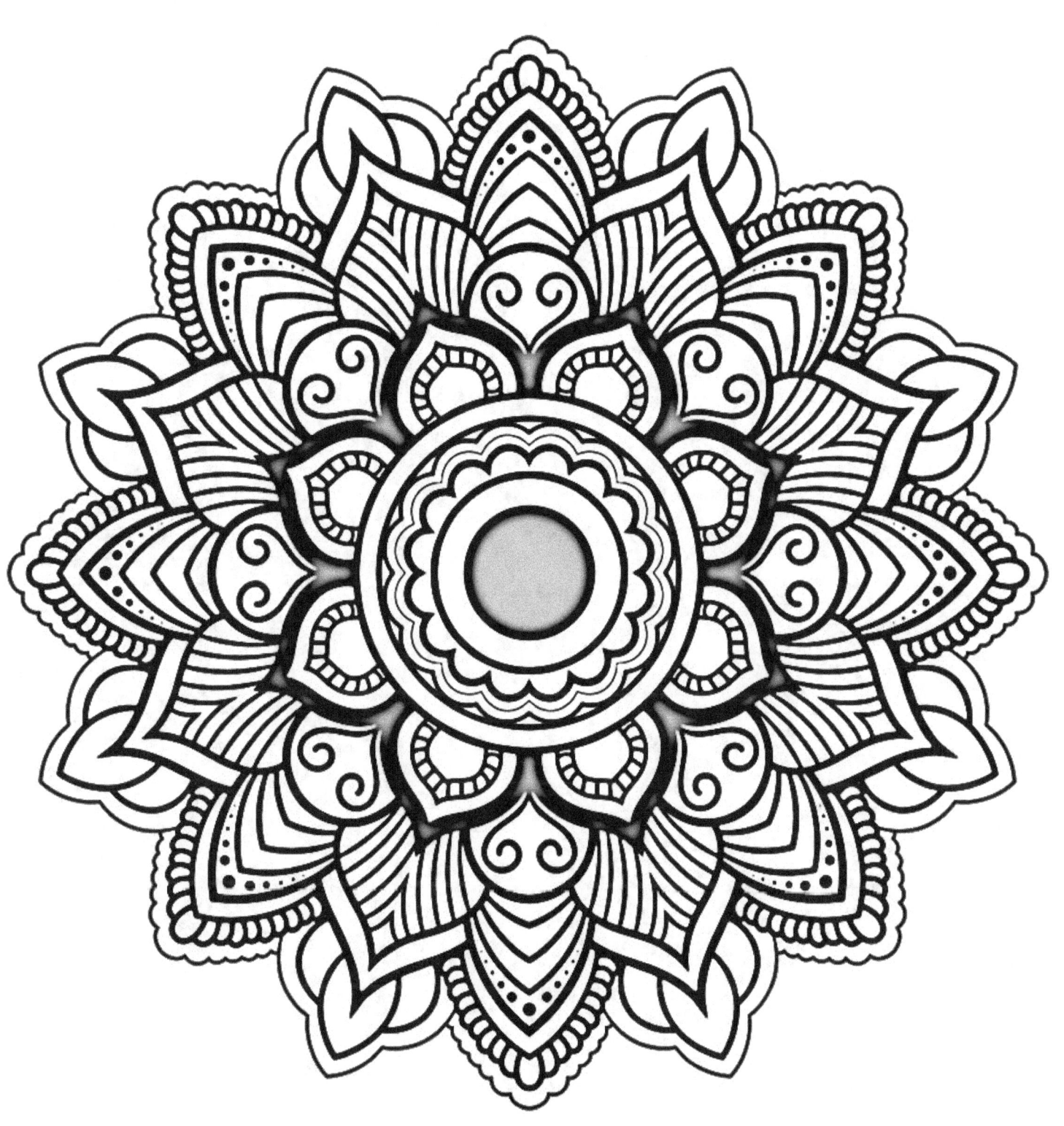

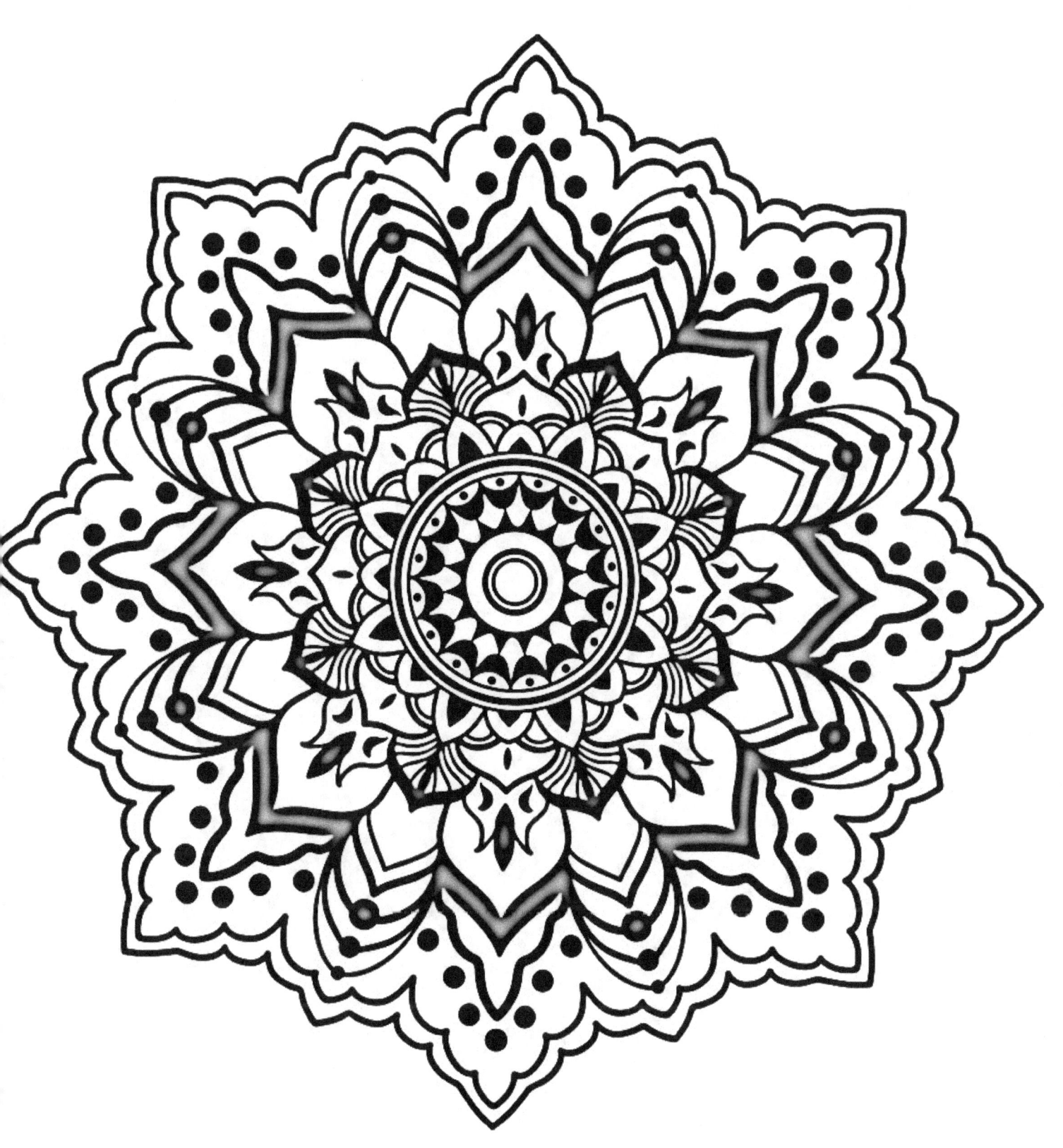

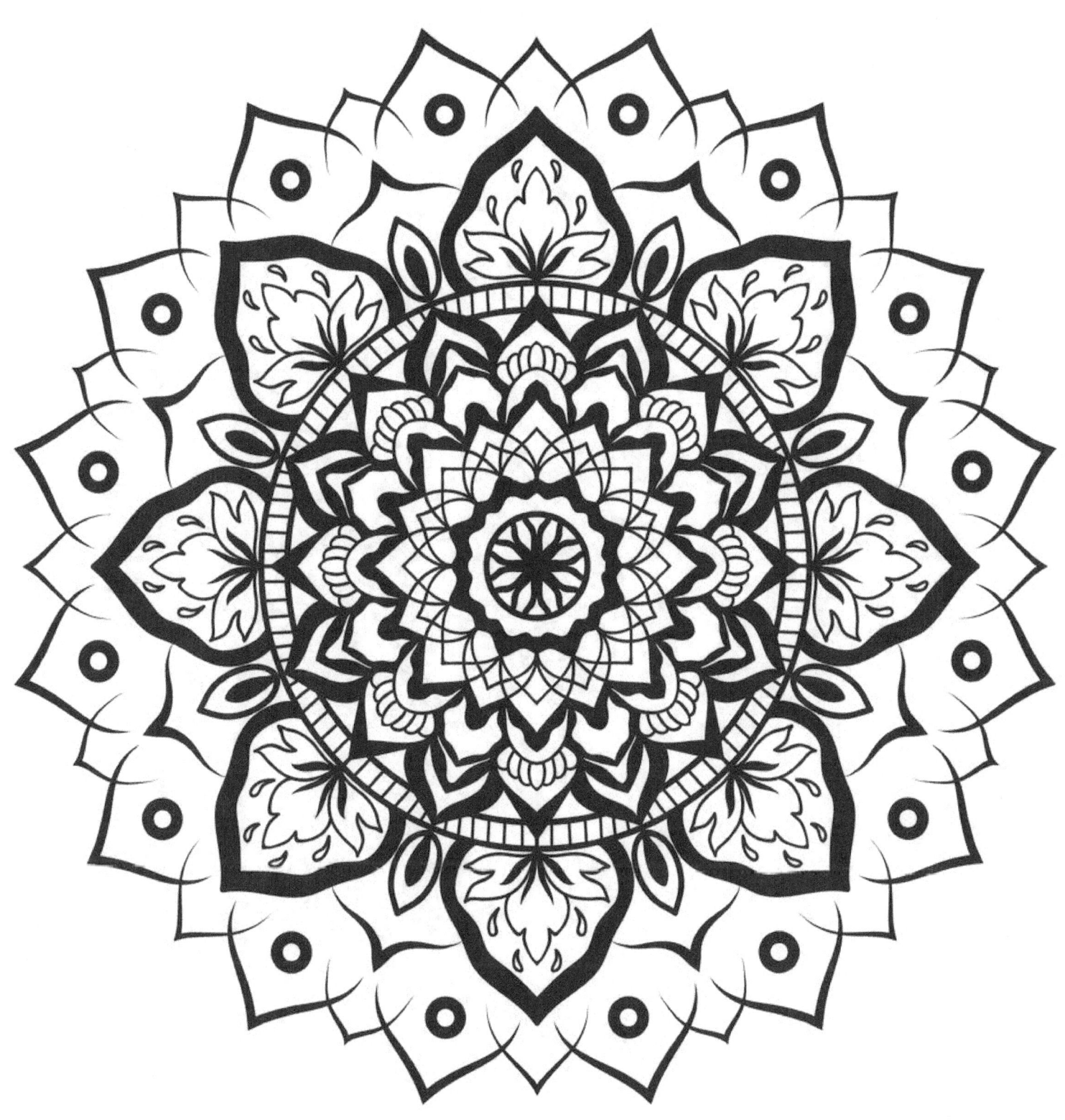

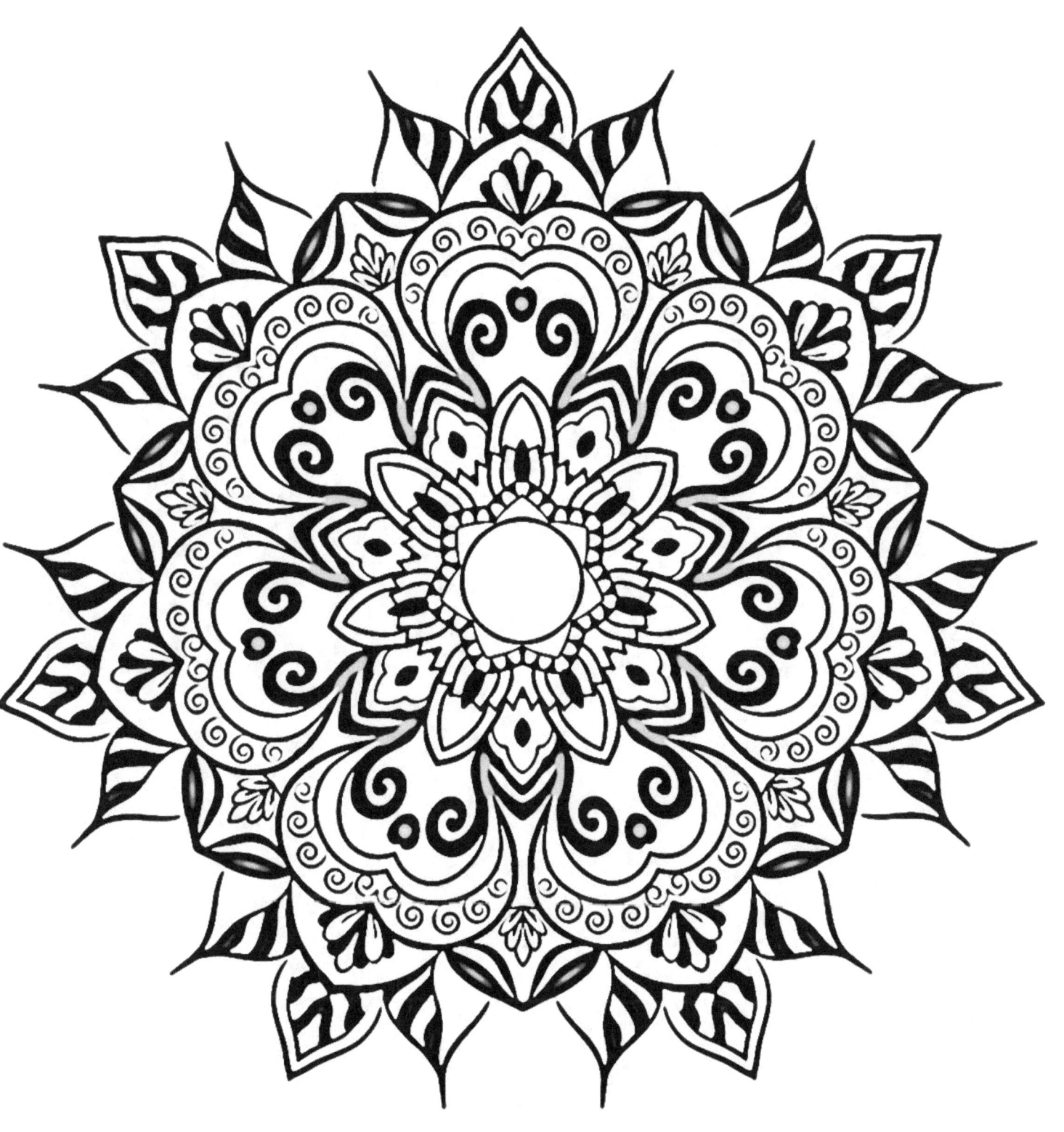